PARADIGMS OF
INDIAN ARCHITECTURE

Centre of South Asian Studies,
School of Oriental and African Studies,
University of London

COLLECTED PAPERS ON SOUTH ASIA

10. Institutions and Ideologies
David Arnold and Peter Robb

11. Local Agrarian Societies in Colonial India
Peter Robb, Kaoru Sugihara, Haruka Yanagisawa

12. Myth and Mythmaking
Julia Leslie

COLLECTED PAPERS ON SOUTH ASIA NO. 13

PARADIGMS OF INDIAN ARCHITECTURE
Space and Time in Representation and Design

Edited by

G.H.R. Tillotson

CURZON

First published in 1998
by Curzon Press
15 The Quadrant, Richmond
Surrey, TW9 1BP

© 1998 G.H.R. Tillotson

Printed in Great Britain by
Biddles Ltd, Guildford and King's Lynn

British Library Cataloguing in Publication Data
A catalogue record for this book is available from the British Library

Library of Congress in Publication Data
A catalogue record for this book has been requested

ISBN 0–7007–0628–3 hbk
ISBN 0–7007–1038–8 pbk

CONTENTS

NOTES ON THE CONTRIBUTORS

Thomas R. Metcalf
Professor of History at the University of California, Berkeley; author of *An Imperial Vision* (Faber and Faber, 1989).

Tapati Guha-Thakurta
Fellow in History at the Centre for Studies in Social Sciences, Calcutta; author of *The Making of a New 'Indian' Art* (CUP, 1992).

G.H.R. Tillotson
Senior Lecturer in South Asian Art at SOAS, University of London; author of *The Tradition of Indian Architecture* (Yale, 1989).

Vidya Dehejia
Curator for Indian and Southeast Asian Art at the Freer Gallery of Art and the Arthur M. Sackler Gallery, Washington, D.C.; author of *Early Buddhist Rock Temples* (London, 1972).

Adam Hardy
Director of *Prasada* at De Montfort University, Leicester; author of *Indian Temple Architecture* (New Delhi, 1994).

Anna L. Dallapiccola
Honorary Professor at the Department of Fine Art, University of Edinburgh; editor of *Vijayanagara: City and Empire* (1985)

Kulbhushan Jain
Professor of Architecture at the School of Architecture in Ahmedabad; author of *Mud Architecture of the Indian Desert* (AADI, 1992).

Sunand Prasad
Partner, Penoyre and Prasad Architects, London; author of *The Havelis of North India* (Royal College of Art, London, 1988).

INTRODUCTION

G.H.R. Tillotson

This is a book about conceptions of Indian architecture: about ways in which India's historical architecture has been—and ways in which it might be—thought about. The writing of India's architectural history has always been problematic. The indigenous tradition of scholarly writing on architecture, embodied in treatises known collectively as *silpa-sastras*, concerns itself with theoretical, esoteric and religious matters; these texts provide little description and critical analysis of extant buildings. Such concerns were established as a domain of art-historical scholarship during the British colonial period, by British pioneer archaeologists and art historians and their Indian associates. Inevitably, the model employed for this exercise was an imported one: it was a matter of applying to Indian material methods and procedures already developed elsewhere. In its formative phase, therefore, the investigation of India's architectural history—even when undertaken by Indians themselves—was substantially foreign in approach. In recent years, the writings of these pioneers of the last century have been subjected to trenchant criticism, not to say deconstruction, as they have been analysed in relation to their own historical and ideological contexts. Attempts have also been made to seek out alternative models for interpreting India's great buildings of the past, models perhaps based more closely on indigenous aesthetics and approaches. Complex in themselves, both parts of this project are being undertaken at a time when the wider field of the humanities has been, to say the least, destabilised by recent developments in cultural theory—notably the advancement of ideas about the relationship between objects and 'discourses' about them—which challenge the status of any text which purports to offer an explicatory guide to events or artifacts of the past.

The contributors to this volume are amongst those who have been most active in the field thus sketchily defined; in the present chapters they summarise and further develop ideas and concerns already signalled in their previous writings. These individuals have been selected and brought together not in order to promote some factitious consensus but, on the contrary, to demonstrate certain divergences within the spectrum. They make up a varied group in a number of

ways. Firstly, they approach the subject from an assortment of
disciplines, since they include historians, art historians and architects;
they vary also in the stance they adopt towards influential theoretical
ideas outside the immediate field. And they differ widely in the subject
matter—the particular buildings, objects or texts—which provide the
terrain of their enquiries. They certainly form no co-ordinated project
team, or homogeneous group. They were brought together in the first
place in the belief that their arguments illuminate each other by
contrast: the juxtaposition draws each into a sharper focus. A secondary
and unexpected consequence is that the approaches of some throw
additional light on the subject-matter or material of others; some
surprising connections emerge across the boundaries of chosen topic
and method. The whole is thus truly more than the sum total of its parts.

The book is meant to serve two functions: it is a means of taking
stock of certain recent developments in the field of Indian art history,
and (more practically) it demonstrates, and explores the tensions
between, a range of possible competing methods within that field. In
addition, it highlights for investigation those emergent themes which
connect the chapters together. These themes (already signalled in the
book's title and subtitle) will be outlined in the final section of this
Introduction following a survey of the contributions to the debate made
by each of the chapters individually. But first, it is necessary to return
to the starting point of that debate, to the problem of the colonial
scholar selecting a model or pattern for understanding. This might be
most clearly illustrated by reviewing one well-known passage from a
seminal text.

James Fergusson's path-breaking *History of Indian and Eastern
Architecture* (1876) opens with a lament that the narrow focus of a
European's education excludes familiarity with the history and culture
of India. In particular he protests that no one has a right to claim
knowledge of architecture who is ignorant of the buildings of India.
The modest purpose of his great work was to begin to set matters right,
to reveal to English readers how India's 'arts are more original and
more varied, and her forms of civilisation present an ever-changing
variety, such as are nowhere else to be found'. His readers soon
discover, however, that at times, for all his enthusiasm, Fergusson
found this originality and variety somewhat baffling. He felt a definite
disquiet, for example, about many 'Dravidian', or south Indian,
temples. He admired the Rajarajeshvara temple at Tanjore (Thanjavur),

which he considered to be built on 'a well-defined and stately plan', but he regretted that it was so unusual:

> The temple at Tiruvalur, about thirty miles west of Madras, contrasts curiously with that at Tanjore in the principles on which it was designed, and serves to exemplify the mode in which, unfortunately, most Dravidian temples were aggregated.

He goes on to explain how a small central shrine standing in a courtyard with a gate, was enclosed within a surrounding courtyard with larger gates, and then subsequently the whole ensemble was enclosed again by a further courtyard with yet larger gates. This method of growth he identified as typical of the 'unfortunate' Dravidian mode:

> As an artistic design, nothing can be worse. The gateways…lose half their dignity from their positions, and the bathos of their decreasing in size and elaboration, as they approach the sanctuary, is a mistake which nothing can redeem. We may admire the beauty of detail…but as an architectural design it is altogether detestable.

There were greater disappointments in store for Fergusson:

> The temple which has been most completely marred by this false system of design is that at Seringham [Srirangam], which is certainly the largest, and if its principle of design could be reversed, would be one of the finest temples in the south of India…
>
> Looked at from a distance…[its] fourteen or fifteen great gate towers cannot fail to produce a certain effect…but even then it can only be by considering them as separate buildings. As parts of one whole, their arrangement is exactly that which enables them to produce the least possible effect… Had the four great outer *gopuras* formed the four sides of a central hall, and the others gone on diminishing, in three or four directions, to the exterior, the effect of the whole would have been increased to a surprising degree.

The eastern half of the Great Temple at Srirangam (Fergusson)

It would be too simplistic a reading of Fergusson to suppose that his only intention in such passages was to disparage: his overall aim was to inspire admiration for Indian architecture, and in cases where he thought this inappropriate, his tone is one of sorrow. He was quite correct in identifying the principle of organisation employed at Tiruvalur and Srirangam as typical of much south Indian temple architecture, particularly under the patronage of the Cholas and later rulers of the region.

What is remarkable about his analysis is his description of that principle as a *'false* system of design', as a 'mistake' which would be better 'reversed'—criticisms which indicate that he had in mind a 'correct' system, too obvious to require explanation, which ought to have been followed. The principle employed certainly makes the temples strange to Western eyes. If one's notion of what a great religious building ought to look like is derived from European cathedrals, then it would be disconcerting to find a tradition where the most impressive elements are placed at the margins, and where high walls create a perplexing maze and deny us a view of the central focus. And it would be a relief to encounter the temple at Thanjavur, for, though also strange in outline, it is at least a single, majestic mass of masonry which one can walk around or enter, with one vast tower providing a main focus: it approximates more closely to a familiar type.

One might be inclined to say that Fergusson missed the point. Though the temple at Thanjavur perhaps provides an exception, the aim of south Indian temple-builders was not generally to leave us standing in wonder at a monolithic mass, but rather to lead the pilgrim (and the architectural historian, for that matter) through a sequence of spaces, on a path that takes him to a concealed sacred centre. Fergusson approached the temples with a predetermined model for religious architecture, and proceeded to judge them against that alien standard; not surprisingly, he found them wanting and—more importantly— failed to discern the qualities of the model which the builders had employed.

That model is not of course the only one ever used in India. The region's long history has seen the development of a great diversity of architectural types. Very different aesthetic principles and systems have governed the design of, say, Medieval temples, Sultanate mosques, Colonial public buildings, and Modernist housing schemes. A part of the task of the art historian is to unravel and to describe those systems, in order to locate the designs of particular buildings within them. One obstacle to that task, as the example of Fergusson shows, is that, no less than the buildings he seeks to understand, the art historian is historically situated: he brings to bear upon his subject preformed ideas about aesthetics and about his discipline which provide a structure or pattern for interpretation. Thus, even the simple list of architectural types given above is open to objection. It might be argued that these types do not represent discrete, self-contained categories, that historically they overlapped and interacted: some of the design principles of Medieval temples can be detected in Sultanate mosques, which in turn provided inspiration for some Colonial public buildings, and (in spite of much rhetoric) there are profound continuities between the Colonial and Modernist periods. Alternatively, the categories could be further subdivided and each shown to contain a diversity of design ideals. They are, in other words, not natural categories, but systems by which art historians order their material, and there is ample scope for disagreement about them. The systems of art historians, like those of architectural designers, are paradigms.

Such problems beset all art history, of course. A further obstacle, more specific to Indian architecture, is that scholarly study of the field has its origins in the British Colonial period, and notably in the work of Fergusson. Even indigenous writers of the nineteenth century, such as Ram Raz and Syed Ahmad Khan, were greatly influenced by Western styles of scholarship. For most of us, the certainties of that period have been overthrown, and its methods questioned; but there is less agreement about what should be put in their place. Sometimes the very process of overturning the inherited colonial discourse appears to pose questions, only to leave them unanswerable.

For example, the account of Fergusson given above concludes that he 'missed the point', and that he mistakenly applied the 'wrong' paradigm. Yet this objection looks very similar to the substance of his own criticism of the south Indian temple-builders: that they mistakenly followed the wrong model. The account therefore places us in the same relationship with respect to Fergusson as that which it identifies between him and Srirangam—one which was deemed to be inadmissible. The passage quoted from Fergusson makes a covert manoeuvre, an implicit appeal to a supposedly transcendent or correct model for architecture; yet the objection to that manoeuvre also replicates it, by making an implicit appeal to a supposedly transcendent model for art history. Much recent cultural theory is concerned to show that what purports to reveal objective reality is merely narrative or discursive device. The theory is not selective, however, and if it is used as a tool to enable us to expose the strategies of Colonial discourse, it will also pre-empt and undermine any account we may offer in its place.

The chapters of the present book explore how systems of design and ideas about aesthetics have informed the ways in which buildings in India have been created and described. That is to say, the book examines patterns of thought which have governed both the construction of architecture in India, and its subsequent interpretation. Against the background of these problems of methodology, the contributors to this volume differ but overlap, both in the approaches which they adopt and in the aspects of the topic which they address.

The historian Thomas Metcalf has long been established as an authority on the political institutions and ideologies of the British Raj; in his book *An Imperial Vision* (1989) he turned to consider their reflection in British scholarly writing on the architecture of India's past, and even in British colonial architecture itself. Though full of original interpretations of particular texts and buildings, this book drew inspiration for its theoretical underpinning from the ideas of Michel Foucault and Edward Said, in particular the former's arguments about the nature of discursive practices and the latter's application of those arguments to the imbalances of power which mark colonialism. Metcalf saw the work of writers such as Fergusson, and the use of supposedly indigenous motifs in imperial architecture, as declarations of mastery over India's cultural past, and suggested that both could be read as undertaken by the British as 'a way to control that past, and hence India's present, for their own purposes'. In Chapter 1 of this book, he pursues this theme, especially in relation to two minor but representative projects: the Viceroy Curzon's gift of a lamp to hang in the Taj Mahal (1905), and the design of the Selangor Secretariat in Kuala Lumpur (1897). In both cases he focuses on the British assumption of authority over the nature of 'Islamic' architecture: in the first case it involved claiming a monopoly of knowledge about a celebrated monument of the past; in the latter it involved exporting to a wholly different context a British construction of how Islamic identity was to be reflected in new architectural design. At the heart of both projects, Metcalf argues, is a method of using the past which differs significantly from those that had been adopted by earlier rulers in India, and which could be said to constitute a recognizably colonial aesthetic.

Tapati Guha-Thakurta, also originally an historian, has worked within a similar theoretical framework as Metcalf but on slightly different subject-matter: her book *The Making of a New 'Indian' Art*

(1992) focused on art, art education and art criticism, chiefly in Bengal around the turn of the century. Amongst other themes, this book charts the challenges to the order established by Fergusson and his contemporaries that were made by a new generation of scholars in the early twentieth century, especially Comaraswamy and Havell, who sought to ground their interpretation of Indian art within indigenous aesthetics. The guiding inspiration is again apparent, however, in her characterisation of this exercise as a 'new phase of Orientalism'. In Chapter 2 of this book she expands on the argument here introduced by Metcalf by examining in detail the methods of the major early archaeologist Alexander Cunningham, particularly in relation to his work on the stupa at Bharhut in the 1870s. She explains how this newly rediscovered monument was made to play a part in a British narrative of India's cultural past, and to yield itself to Western methods of scientific investigation. In the later sections of the chapter, Guha-Thakurta turns to consider the treatment of this same monument in the writings of Bengali scholars, and particularly of Rakhaldas Banerjee (1914). Here, contentions over how to read the monument as evidence of the past are located firmly in the context of emergent nationalism. To earlier quarrels (especially with Rajendralal Mitra) about the results which a generally accepted method produces is added a new contested domain: the question of method itself, of literary genre, and of the kind of past that is to be retrieved, and for whom.

My own chapter also focuses on the British period but examines a different mode of representation: not the verbal mode of art-historical analysis but visual representation in painting. This complicates the interpretative layer since the mode of showing is itself aesthetically constructed. British images are contrasted with Indian ones, and the two are shown to reflect not just different pictorial conventions but different priorities and concerns about architecture itself. I argue that the comparison can suggest to us reasons for preferring a particular path by which to approach the buildings themselves.

Similar issues are explored in another very different context by Vidya Dehejia: her chapter considers the representation of space, movement and time in the narrative pictorial art of ancient India, focusing on Buddhist sites including Bharhut, Sanchi and Ajanta. As in other, recent and related studies by Dehejia, she is here concerned to show the dominance of space over time in this art. In spite of the importance of time in the stories that are illustrated, the organizing principle in their representation appears to be space. The episodes of a tale are arranged according to where, not when, they occurred in the narrative sequence. At first sight, this looks like a reversal of the findings of the preceding chapter: there, some Indian depictions of buildings were found to be focused less on their spatial context than on an experience of them through time; here, a sequence of events is depicted not chronologically but according to a logic that is spatial. If Indian depictions of the most spatial and immovable of objects turn out to have a strong narrative content, it seems nothing less than perverse that narrative art should suppress, comparatively, the element of time. But, as Dehejia shows, the perversity arises from the expectations of the modern viewer. Here (as in the previous case), the artist has placed the emphasis on a conception needing to be communicated, rather than a perception, already familiar and taken for granted. In both cases, that treatment gives rise to a tension between space and time.

These early chapters, then, do not address Indian architecture directly. Rather, they explore how architecture and space have been understood and represented, verbally and visually, according to colonial and indigenous paradigms. The later chapters are less concerned with secondary representation. More empirical in method, they suggest ways in which buildings can be said to present their own clues to understanding them.

Thus, Adam Hardy boldly dismisses the claims of the literary tradition of the *sastras* as an explicatory guide to temple architecture, and argues that the temples themselves reveal the principles of their design: that their external walls can be read as a kind of grammar for their own interpretation. The method deployed here, Hardy has worked out on a larger scale in his book *Indian Temple Architecture* (1994). Underlying the bewildering complexity and diversity of temple forms, he argues, is a clear logic—a set of basic building blocks and of principles of composition which, once identified, enable one to classify (indeed almost predict) any given example. The process of multiplication by which the constituent parts increase, Hardy sees as a process of emanation—of forms emerging from within others. What this implies is that any given temple could be seen as an arrested moment in such a process of emanation, implying both endless increase and an origin in nothingness.

The further discussion of temple architecture by Anna Dallapiccola is focused on Vijayanagara (where the author has been a leading member of the Research Project). In this chapter, the whole site is seen to contribute to a complex iconographical scheme, of which it provides itself the best document, although the key to unlock it, she argues, is a proper understanding of the motives of royal patronage. Looking back to a major preoccupation of Part One of this book, Dallapiccola finds it necessary to clear the ground of 19th-century scholarship, with its prejudices against the late and therefore supposedly decadent forms of the Vijayanagara temples. Like Dehejia, she concentrates on the narrative sculpture which is carried by architecture. Thus, moving beyond the aesthetic concerns of the West, and examining the sculpture closely, she argues for the emergence in the sixteenth century of a distinctive Vijayanagara imperial style.

Similarly based on close visual scrutiny, Kulbhushan Jain's chapter moves the discussion into the realms of domestic architecture. He concentrates on Rajasthan, and the aesthetic, social and climatic factors which govern the architectural forms. India's secular tradition has been comparatively neglected. It has begun to receive some belated and welcome attention in recent years, so that Jain is no longer alone, but he has been an important pioneer in this field. His approach generally, and in this chapter specifically, is recognizably that of a professional architect. In the first place, he is concerned to learn about India's past traditions not least for the benefits to be derived for current practice. He is no copyist, and like other architects he is anxious to avoid pastiche, but he is also alert to the possibility of relearning once familiar lessons, particularly on matters such as climate control. His architectural training also emerges in the belief that aesthetic expression arises primarily from function. He qualifies this belief but is reluctant to abandon it, and so here again is the mark of the architectural modernist's disdain for surface form. This lineage, too, he recognizes, and he therefore concludes that a modernist paradigm, though often applied, is ultimately unhelpful in analysing India's traditional domestic architecture.

Some of these threads are taken up in the final chapter by Sunand Prasad—also an architect. Prasad examines two alternative paradigms for domestic architecture in comparatively recent times—the Colonial and the indigenous—assessing the complex social forces involved in making choices between them. The study compares a district of the old city of Shahjabanabad with one of the more fashionable residential 'colonies' of southern New Delhi. The differences are not only of morphology but of meaning and use. Here too are potential lessons for architects, and some indeed have tried to learn them; but a morphology is more easily recaptured than a meaning, and Prasad concludes that in spite of recent efforts the indigenous paradigm is in terminal decline. Even this, however, does not make its lessons obsolete, and in spite of his pessimism, Prasad sustains the note sounded by Jain: in this last section we have moved from paradigms for understanding India's past towards paradigms for building for its future.

Though diverse, the coverage of these chapters collectively is not comprehensive. It is not for a moment supposed that the book covers all important Indian architecture (or that that would be possible). The close attention paid to particular groups of buildings—to their design principles and their interpretation—leaves many other possible paradigms unexplored. The chapters are united, however, by their common endeavour to consider how to practise the analysis of architecture in India in a post-Colonial and post-structuralist intellectual context. The context is post-Colonial because we are now sufficiently removed historically from the purposes and methods of that era to examine them in some perspective. It is post-structuralist in the sense that all of the writers are alert to the problems of the location of the speaker, the problems of attempting to arrive at one 'correct' vision or account.

The chapters are further connected by certain linking themes. Indian architecture itself provides the first and most apparent of these, despite a considerable diversity in the perspectives from which it is approached. The first two chapters (Section I: The Monument Described) are concerned with verbal accounts or analyses of Indian architecture in the colonial period. The chapters of Section II (The Depicted Place) shift the emphasis from verbal to visual representations of architecture, as each is concerned primarily with images of structures or of space; they deal successively with depictions *of* tombs and mosques, and depictions *on* stupas. Despite these subtle changes in perspective, and the general shift to the visual domain, the buildings themselves provide common ground with the preceding section, since Mughal architecture is the main concern of both Chapters 1 and 3, and ancient Buddhist monuments of Chapters 2 and 4. In Part Two, India's historic buildings assume an even more central place. First, Chapters 5 and 6 examine forms from India's sacred architecture in the Hindu tradition. The two chapters constitute Section III: The Built Form. Finally, Chapters 7 and 8 in the concluding Section IV (The Inhabited Space), consider the organization of space in Indian domestic architecture contrasting traditional and more recent models.

Another important thematic concern is indicated by the title word 'paradigms', here meant in the sense of 'patterns' or 'models' and encompassing both systems of production or design, and styles of subsequent understanding. The structure of the book reverses the sequence thus implied. The 'subsequent understandings' —as we saw in the case of Fergusson—add a further layer of interpretation, whose refracting properties have to be understood first if we are to try and focus on the paradigms of design. Thus the chapters of Part One discuss various representations as indicators of understandings, while the chapters of Part Two endeavour, by more empirical means, to approach the originating principles of design.

It is perhaps not surprising that a series of essays on paradigms of architecture should be further linked by the themes of space and time, but it may be worthwhile drawing attention to the modulations in these themes through the book's course. To begin with—since the chapters of Section I are concerned with the colonial period—space and time are markers of *disjunction*: specifically, the separation in time between historical architecture and the colonial discourses about them; and the transformation of ambient space, as buildings which served the needs of historical empires become relics surviving as monuments in a colonial one. In the chapters of Section II, the themes of space and time reappear in a form somewhat different but no less important, since the indigenous kinds of visual representation that are discussed turn out to be, in ways crucial to their functioning, *narrative* images; they encode experiences not just in space but in time. The chapters on Hindu temples in Section III explore ways in which a sense of time is contained within the very forms of sacred architecture. The link which temples make between the temporal world of man and that of the gods is well known; more particularly in focus here, are the idea of sequence, which arises when architecture is seen as a depiction of emanation (Chapter 5); and the manner in which, at the site discussed in Chapter 6, a link with mythic time is mapped out through sacred geography. The chapters of the concluding Section IV are focused on the organization of space in domestic architecture, particularly as this has altered in recent times; and the comparison made in the final chapter between traditional and imported paradigms returns us to the disjunctions in space and time with which we began.

Chapter One

PAST AND PRESENT:
TOWARDS AN AESTHETICS OF COLONIALISM

Thomas R. Metcalf

On 19 April 1905, Lord Curzon, then Viceroy of India, wrote to Lord Cromer, British Proconsul in Egypt:

> I want to give a beautiful hanging lamp of Saracenic design to be hung [in the Taj Mahal] above the cenotaphs of Shah Jahan and his queen in the upper mausoleum. The original chain is still hanging from the centre of the great dome, but the lamp has long disappeared. I have been trying for years to get the people here to give me a design, but have failed. I turn therefore to Cairo, where my recollection is that some very beautiful lamps still hang in the Arab mosques. If I can get a good design I would propose to have one of these reproduced in silver at Cairo. The style of the Taj you know to be what we call Indo-Saracenic, which is really Arabic, with flowering substituted for geometric patterns.[1]

What is striking about this passage—other than the fact two such powerful imperial luminaries as Lords Curzon and Cromer are corresponding about lamps—is the sense of mastery, control and self-confidence than emanates from it, and that not on a matter of high policy, but of aesthetics. Curzon knew what the Taj was, how it should be decorated, and who had the responsibility for its ornamentation (Fig. 1). We shall return presently to the Taj lamp—which still hangs where Curzon placed it—but let us first notice two other—seemingly different—structures of the same years. One is the Victoria Memorial Hall, Madras, designed by H.C. Irwin in 1906. Built of red sandstone, this building endeavoured to recreate the style of Akbar's capital of Fatehpur Sikri, a thousand miles to the north. The second, a thousand miles to the east of Madras, is the Selangor Secretariat in Kuala Lumpur, Malaya, completed in 1897 (Fig. 2). Its architectural style was described at the time variously as 'Arabesque judiciously mixed with Indian detail', and, by the architect C.E. Spooner, simply as 'Mahometan'.

What is it, one must ask, that binds together as distinctively colonial these three diverse building enterprises—the Taj lamp, the Madras Memorial, and the Selangor Secretariat? In what ways can they be seen as manifesting a set of aesthetic values at all different from those of earlier Indian rulers? How is Curzon's search for a lamp for the Taj different, say, from Firuz Shah Tughlaq's removal in the fourteenth century of a Mauryan pillar from Meerut to his new capital at Kotla Firuz Shah? Is the British modelling of the Madras museum on Akbar's capital at all different from the Vijayanagara rulers' emulation of the architectural styles of the Cholas, or the eighteenth-century Travancore raja Martanda Varma's use in painting and architecture of the styles of *his* predecessors, that is, of Vijayanagara and its successor Nayak kingdoms? At one level, of course, the answer is obvious. The British as colonial rulers, as I have argued elsewhere, saw in the use of Indian

Fig.1 Lord Curzon's lamp in the Taj Mahal (OIOC; British Library)

styles a way to affirm their legitimacy as rulers. As the architect William Emerson, a foremost designer of Saracenic structures, put it, the British should follow the example of those whom they had supplanted as conquerors, the Mughals, who had 'seized upon the art indigenous to the countries they conquered, adapting it to suit their own needs and ideas'. Indeed, argued the Madras governor, Lord Napier, in 1870, the Indian government ought 'to consider whether the Mussulman form might not be adopted generally as the official style of architecture'. Throughout the subsequent half-century the British endeavoured to represent themselves, and their empire, as 'Indian' through the patronage of 'Saracenic' forms.[2]

Yet matters are not so simple. Earlier rulers too, whether the Mughals or those of Vijayanagara, were not averse to appropriating the politically-charged forms of their predecessors as a way of legitimising their own regimes. Firuz Shah surely did not drag an Asokan column all the way from Meerut to Delhi simply for his amusement. Though he did not know of its third-century B.C. origins, this massive stone shaft, with its roots in the ancient past, and its association with the mythic heroes of antiquity, still served (or was meant to serve) an important purpose—that of giving Firuz Shah's inept and tottering regime a status, at least in the emperor's own eyes, that it otherwise lacked. Jahangir too erected in the Allahabad fort a Mauryan pillar bearing inscriptions by Asoka, Samudragupta, and other ancient rulers; and he added to these his own name with full regnal titles and lineage back to Timur. Most importantly, he erected this pillar several months before Akbar died while he was himself still heir apparent. Jahangir's act thus served a double purpose: of affirming at once the legitimacy of the Mughal dynasty, as heir to the illustrious predecessors whose inscriptions the pillar contained, as well as his own personal claim to the throne.[3]

Curzon, nevertheless, was not Jahangir. One critical difference is to be found perhaps, not so much in the *purpose* for which Indic architectural elements were used, but in the *way* they were deployed. One must, that is, look at the underlying sets of assumptions about 'India', about 'architecture', and about 'history', that shaped British Indian building as compared with those of pre-colonial Indian rulers. This is obviously a complex subject about which it is unwise to make easy generalisations. A case could be made, however, for the argument that, by and large, Indian rulers participated in an on-going indigenous architectural tradition. This made available to them an array of forms and styles which they could rework imaginatively, but which confined them within certain modes appropriate to their set time and place in India. Contrary to the accepted view in most scholarly writing since the mid-nineteenth century, Akbar, for instance, as he built Fatehpur-Sikri, surely did not self-consciously deal out architectural elements labelled 'Muslim' and 'Hindu' in order to create for his political purposes a 'synthesis' or 'syncrectism' of the two religions. The vision, for instance, of the Diwan-i-Khas, as containing, as H.H. Cole wrote, an interior column 'thoroughly Hindu' in its outline and details, but covered with 'Mahometan' decorative carving, is one that is wholly British, and wholly colonial.[4]

In his building enterprises, Akbar participated instead in a regional architectural tradition of the sixteenth century. Its forms are to be found in the neighbouring, and contemporaneous, sites of Fatehpur-Sikri, Datia and Gwalior, and were employed alike by rulers of the Hindu and Muslim faiths. To be sure, powerful men, such as Akbar and Jahangir or the Vijayanagara emperors, might endeavour to associate their reigns with the glories of past kingdoms by stylistic emulation, by the appropriation of objects, or by an exaggeration of forms.[5] A vast scale of building announced a ruler's intent to surpass the work of his predecessors. But these monarchs all worked from within a distinctive set of aesthetic conventions—about architecture, about the past, and about how the past was meant to inform royal building—that set them apart from their successors, the British, whose building activities in India were shaped by a wholly different set of assumptions.

One way of capturing part of the difference might be to say that Indian artists and designers endeavoured to make the past, seen as flexible and fluid, into the present, while for the British their chief objective was to make the present appear to be the past. Vishakha Desai's study of copying in painting offers some suggestive insights. In her view, when eighteenth-century artists modelled their work on earlier Bundi paintings, they followed the original compositions and iconographical styles, and then altered clothing, furniture and architectural elements to reflect contemporary taste. Nothing else changed. The paintings took this shape not because the artist was trapped in some unchanging 'immemorial' tradition, nor were they the product of an unsuccessful attempt to recreate the past. Rather, seeing the present as an extension of the past, the artist endeavoured by an exercise of imaginative interpretation to synchronise past and present in his work, and so evoke the correct emotion in the viewer. When, in the early nineteenth century, artists began to copy earlier Mughal paintings for British patrons, however, the situation was dramatically reversed.

Explicitly instructed to *copy* such works, the artist could no longer exercise the freedom of updating clothing, furniture or architecture. Instead he was meant to create consciously archaised works that would delude British buyers into thinking that they had purchased a Mughal original. The tie to a glorious past remained—in the desire of the British to procure works of their illustrious Mughal predecessors—but the whole relation to that past was different. No longer was it to flow into the present. It was a past seen as past, from which the British stood apart. Now, for the first time, as he sought to make the present appear to be the past, was the copyist painter truly confined by tradition. It was, however, British, not Indian tradition, that confined him.[6]

One must beware, of course, of attributing these differing perceptions to some inherent difference between India and Britain, or arguing that there exists some essentially 'Indian' mode of appropriating the past. The typology of the 'present' as a centre into which the past always runs, and which alone gives meaning to the 'past', is not a mode of thought uniquely Indic. It is found elsewhere, above all in Europe itself, before the rise in the Enlightenment of an historicist, or linear, consciousness. In this earlier view, the present was not simply a link in a chain of empty events, but simultaneously that which has been and that which will be. Early Italian and Flemish painters of the Nativity, for instance, clearly expressed this vision in paintings that, without incongruity, dressed the Holy Family in contemporary garb, while setting the scenic backdrop in the painter's own locale, Tuscany or Flanders, say, not Palestine. Only from the seventeenth century, or later, does the past become a 'foreign country' cut off from ourselves and our time.[7]

Informed by novel, and peculiarly modern European, perspectives on time and the past, the colonial aesthetic thus involved a self-conscious distancing of the British from India and its past. To be sure, the British often imagined themselves within the on-going traditions of Indian design. James Ransome, consulting architect to the Government of India, in 1905, for instance, without any sense of incongruity described the tomb of Salim Chishti at Fatehpur-Sikri together with Swinton Jacob's 1880 Albert Hall in Jaipur as representative samples of 'Saracenic work'.[8] Indeed, the very use of the term 'Indo-Saracenic' by the British to describe their own building, as well as that which had gone before, carried with it the implication that their structures were but the latest in a long line of buildings constructed in a similar style.

Yet the British always ordered Indic elements in new ways, and for novel purposes, with scant regard for the contexts in which they were rooted. The ritual of the great British Indian durbars is suggestive. Although Disraeli, when he made Queen Victoria Empress of India, exulted that now, as his viceroy Lord Lytton put it, the monarch would 'sit in the seat of the great Mogul', nevertheless the accompanying decoration and ritual were all inspired by European feudalism, and represented a British conception of India as medieval and its princes as feudal vassals. In his 1903 durbar, repudiating Lytton's 'medieval' idiom, Curzon sought to utilise the 'familiar and even sacred' forms of 'the East'. As he proudly proclaimed, the entire arena was 'built and decorated exclusively in the Mogul, or Indo-Saracenic style'. Yet Curzon refused to sanction an exchange of presents, or *nazrs*, which had formed the central binding element of pre-colonial durbars. Instead he had each prince in turn mount the dais and offer a message of congratulation to the new king-emperor. Curzon then simply shook hands with the chief as he passed by. Incorporation and inclusion, so powerfully symbolised by *khillat* and *nazr*, had given way, despite the Mughal scenery and the pretence, to a wholly colonial ritual.[9]

In architecture, a similar sense of distance and manipulation informed at once Britain's own building in India and the British appropriation of its historic buildings. Swinton Jacob's six-volume 1890 'Jeypore Portfolio of Architectural Details', for instance, brought together for British Indian buildings 375 plates of architectural drawings, illustrating an array of elements from historic buildings throughout northern India. In similar fashion, during the later nineteenth century, and especially during Lord Curzon's viceroyalty, the British meticulously identified India's major historic sites, and preserved them through the Archaeological Survey of India. Yet none of this took appreciable account of the historical context in which such structures came into being. Design elements the British liked—such as the arch and dome, together with various plinths, copings, capitals, brackets and so forth, illustrated in Jacob's compendium—were, in their view, available for any purpose and could be employed anywhere. For the colonial builder, that is, the elements of Indian architecture represented not an aesthetic tradition within which he worked, but an external 'Oriental' aesthetic, whose elements, at the deepest level, were similar and interchangeable.

Of course the British were not unaware of India's lengthy and complex past. To the contrary, they were determined from the beginning of their rule to give to this land a 'proper' history. For this purpose India's historic architecture served at once as text and signifier. As the pioneer architectural historian James Fergusson wrote, the architecture of India was a 'great stone book, in which each tribe and race has written its annals and recorded its faith'. Fergusson himself, and after him the Archaeological Survey, set on foot a minute and detailed study of India's monuments with the objective of compiling a 'systematic record and description' of all historic structures, and so placing them in proper chronological order. Nor was this history without a moral. For these ancient structures, so the British argued, told a tale of India's decline from an ancient era of greatness, associated above all with the Buddhist period, to a 'corrupt' and 'degenerate' idolatry associated with medieval Hinduism. Almost always the triumphs of Indian art were ascribed to the influence of foreign invaders. As Curzon told the Asiatic Society in 1900, India's great artistic achievements were all 'exotics imported into this country in the train of conquerors, who had learnt their architectural lessons in Persia, in Central Asia, in Arabia, in Afghanistan'. The British themselves were only 'borne to India on the crest of a later but similar wave'.[10]

Nevertheless, despite this obsession with history, in practice the process of preservation abstracted monuments from their historical context. In archaeology the colonial aesthetic demanded that ancient monuments be preserved, preferably in garden surroundings, in a half-ruined state. The aesthetic was one of the 'picturesque', in which romantic notions of 'grandeur' and 'fallen majesty' were linked to a keen sense of the British role in preserving these structures in the proper state of arrested decay. Mute witnesses to a past whose achievements had been superseded by those of the Raj, India's antiquities could not be allowed to crumble into oblivion, nor could they be put to use, either by the British themselves or by the local people. A district official was slapped down when he proposed outfitting Tirumal Nayak's palace at Madurai as government offices, while Curzon spoke disapprovingly of devotees being allowed annually to whitewash the tombs of saints in Bijapur. He insisted that, once the government had saved these structures from 'destructive carelessness and the uncultured neglect' of the British, 'we were not going to hand them back to the dirt and defilement of Asiatic religious practices'. Indeed, as he told the Asiatic Society in 1900, 'a race like our own, who are themselves foreigners, are in a sense better fitted to guard, with a dispassionate and impartial zeal, the relics of different ages, and of sometimes antagonistic beliefs, than might be the descendants of the warring races of the votaries of the rival creeds'.[11]

So thoroughly did the British tear India's monuments from their historic connections, that they never even considered preserving intact entire districts or neighbourhoods in India's cities. In 1912, New Delhi, for instance, was set down next to the seventeenth-century Mughal capital of Shahjahanabad, now called 'Old Delhi'. But the British objective in doing so was only to associate their Raj with that of its Indian predecessor. The fate of that older urban centre was of no concern to them. Indeed, the British themselves had demolished large chunks of Shahjahanabad for reasons of security after the 1857 revolt, and subsequently tore out further tracts as they drove the new railway lines through the city. In addition, over time the city's *mohallas* (neighbourhoods) and *havelis* (mansions) became transformed in character. Once the splendid residences of wealthy princes whose harems, dependants and storehouses covered vast areas focused around ornately-decorated courtyards, these structures were subdivided, sold and taken over by squatters and petty shopkeepers as the old Mughal élite became ever more impoverished; many over time even became centres of small-scale manufacturing. Even British surveys of these historic structures were not accompanied by any measures to preserve them. Gordon Sanderson, for instance, in 1916 consigned most of Delhi's old tombs and *havelis* to a category of decayed and 'dilapidated' structures, allowed to remain 'monuments of interest' so long as they 'keep together'.[12] Nostalgia for a 'picturesque' old Delhi is a very recent phenomenon.

Such a strategy contrasts not only with the preservation, and renewal, over centuries of such contemporaneous Asian capitals as Isfahan, but even with French colonial practice, above all in Lyautey's Morocco. There, in the years after 1912, under the influence of the ideals of 'associationism', French planners, while erecting ordered colonial cities for themselves (the *nouvelle ville*), also carefully preserved, in their entirety, indigenous urban forms, above all the *medinas* of the old cities of Fez, Marrakesh and Rabat. To be sure, in the process, the French constructed a notion of Moroccan culture, with the *medina* that represented it, as frozen in a 'picturesque' past. By its very nature too, the act of defining another's cultural heritage, arrogant and patronising, made manifest the authority of the colonial regime. Moroccans had no voice in these decisions. Though at one level no more than a romantic vision of the exotic, counterposed to the 'modern' French colonial towns, still, as Gwendolyn Wright has written in her study of French colonial urbanism, the preservation of a city such as Fez testifies to a sensitivity, 'an awareness of cultural particularities', perhaps to an 'aesthetic of pluralism', not found in British India.[13] One might argue, of course, that Delhi had been too battered by war, invasion and revolt over the years since the early eighteenth century for its preservation to be a feasible undertaking. Nevertheless, British indifference to the living city of 'old' Delhi is striking when one considers the loving attention lavished upon deserted cities such as Fatehpur-Sikri and Mandu. Only as a ruin, set in a romantic garden, and given over to tourists, could the British accommodate India's historic sites. Despite the work of James Fergusson and the Archaeological Survey, one might say, the colonial aesthetic in India remained essentially detached from the country's past.

One might, then, return to two of the monuments with which we began—the Taj Mahal and the Selangor Secretariat. They have, a critic might insist, little in common. Yet both tell us much about the way the British, from within the confines of a colonial aesthetic, sought to make sense of the past and of the present. Even though the Selangor Secretariat is not in India at all, but in the Malayan capital of Kuala Lumpur, it still remains intimately connected to India. At one level the connection is simply that of the designer. C.E. Spooner, Selangor State Engineer during the 1890s, though he never served in India itself, had spent some fifteen years employed by the Public Works Department in nearby Ceylon—an experience that presumably taught him what a properly 'Oriental' architecture ought to consist of. Hence, when the official Selangor government architect, A.C. Norman, submitted a design for the new building in a 'classic Renaissance' style, Spooner rejected it in favour of a structure in what he called the 'Mahometan' style.[14] But the question remains: *why* should Spooner do this? After all, the Mughals had never ruled Malaya, and its sultans, though Muslim, had never employed Indic or 'Saracenic' forms. Indeed, there existed very little monumental architecture of any sort in pre-colonial Malaya. Consequently, with no models close at hand, Spooner, with his assistant R.A. Bidwell, had to invent his 'Mahometan' style as he went along. The Selangor Secretariat, with other Kuala Lumpur structures of similar character, thus mixed north Indian elements, like the platform-based cupolas or *chattris*, with horseshoe arches and bands of colour derived from North Africa and Spain, and imaginative features such as elongated spirelets somewhat reminiscent of Ottoman Turkey. The copper-clad clock-tower, lacking any Islamic precedent, was of course wholly colonial, and idiosyncratic in its design.

Such an architecture clearly did not, unlike its counterpart in India, create a past for the British in Malaya, or link their regime to that of some illustrious predecessor. There were no such predecessors; such architectural forms had no past in Malaya. The British sought rather

Fig. 2 The Selangor Secretariat, Kuala Lumpur (photo. Thomas R. Metcalf)

with these buildings to create for Malaya a diffuse 'Mahometan' past, but one defined by Orientalist fancy, not by local usage. All Muslim forms anywhere, that is, could evoke the 'Orient', and so could equally well represent and constitute what was for the British the central fact about Malaya: that, despite the immense number of Indians and Chinese who, along with the British, had come to exploit its resources of tin and rubber, this country was a Malay land; that being Muslim was a prominent part of being Malay; and that that 'Muslimness' should take architectural shape through certain forms that the British, largely on the basis of their experience in India, had determined were properly 'Muslim'.

Even more than in India itself, in consequence, colonial building was in Malaya detached from the land and its past. The distinctive character of this aesthetic—at once wholly colonial and wholly modern—can perhaps best be appreciated by contrasting the design of Malay's pre-colonial mosques with those erected under the British. Indigenous Malayan mosque design was extremely varied in character. Kampung Laut, for instance, erected in the early eighteenth century in Kelantan in the far northeast, was constructed of rich dark wood in a local style of interlocking pieces, while the contemporaneous Masjid Tenkara, at the opposite end of the country in Malacca, was characterised by the use of square sloping roofs joined by a pagoda, presumably of Chinese influence. In the early nineteenth century, as the populations of the coastal towns grew ever more cosmopolitan, the local Muslims devised ever more eclectic styles of mosque architecture. Some, originally from south India, built shrines that unselfconsciously joined together Corinthian pilasters, stepped pagoda-style minarets, and domes. The most striking of these early nineteenth-century structures is undoubtedly the 1846 Hajjah Fatimah mosque in Singapore, whose single prominent minaret recalls, and was presumably modelled on, the nearby Anglican cathedral. In sum, until well into the colonial era there existed no sense that domes, arches, arabesques and all the rest were needed to make a building Muslim.

All this was to change as the British, after the conquest of Malaya in the 1870s, endeavoured to enforce upon its people, above all its sultans, an 'appropriate' architecture that would mark out the land as Muslim. The central mosque of Kuala Lumpur itself (1909) is perhaps representative. Its design incorporates an open courtyard, with three domes and two minarets, predominantly north Indian in character, together with bands of colour and scalloped arches drawn from non-Indian sources. The whole fitted harmoniously into the larger Kuala

Lumpur architectural scheme, which was not surprising since the structure was designed by the local British architect, A.B. Hubback. But the British vision of Islam, and of Muslim architecture, could not be wholly contained within the chaste forms of north Indian design. Hubback himself designed what is by far the most lavish colonial mosque in Malaya—that of Kuala Kangsar (1915) in the tin-rich state of Perak. With its enormous dome and towering minarets, brilliantly painted a golden colour, its horseshoe arches that recall Andalusia, and the glowing red glass embedded in the base of the dome, this structure evoked a British fantasy of Islam wholly separate from the living world of the Malay peninsula.

In conclusion, we might return to the Taj Mahal. The Taj always posed enormous problems for the British. It was, simply, too beautiful, too magnificent, too overwhelming. British travellers, from the late eighteenth century onward, could hardly find word sufficient to praise it. William Hodges, for instance, wrote of the Taj that:

> it possesses a degree of beauty, from the perfection of the materials and the excellence of the workmanship, which is only surpassed by its grandeur, extent, and general magnificence.... The fine materials, the beautiful forms, and the symmetry of the whole, with the judicious choice of situation, far surpasses anything I ever beheld.[15]

Certainly, some of the appeal of the Taj was due to the way it incorporated European aesthetic values such as balance and symmetry, together with its 'picturesque' location in a parklike garden, and its romantic associations with Shah Jahan and his queen. Yet the attraction of the Taj was inseparable from the idea of the 'Orient'. As the architect William Emerson wrote:

> Its romantic situation, dazzling brilliancy, excessive elaboration, and the...lavish display of wealth in its ornamentation, make it beyond all others a place in which a cold-blooded Caucasian can perhaps realize somewhat of the poetical and luxurious feeling of the voluptuous Easterns.[16]

The custom of a moonlight viewing, as it was no doubt meant to be, further enhanced this exoticising effect. In so far as the Taj represented for its European visitors an idealised 'Orient', detached from India, it expressed the values that shaped a colonial aesthetic. From the Kuala Kangsar mosque to the Taj Mahal was, in the end, but a small step.

Lord Curzon as Viceroy made the Taj his obsession. He visited Agra annually, and, as he himself proudly acknowledged, personally supervised and gave orders on every single detail of its restoration. He was determined, above all, to make the Taj resemble his vision of what it ought to have been like. He had the 'garish English flowers' removed, and rows of cypresses planted instead, ignoring critics who pointed out that their dense mass would interfere with the view of the building. He insisted that the guardians of the tomb, in place of their 'very dingy' ordinary garments, should wear 'the traditional garb of Mogul days'; and so he fitted them out with white suits with a green scarf and a badge. 'It is', he said, 'what Akbar himself always wore'.[17] And he set out to find a lamp for the tomb chamber.

Given the enduring British view of the Taj as not only a Mughal, but a 'Saracenic' and an 'Oriental' structure, it is not surprising that Curzon looked to Cairo for his lamp. But his vision of where an appropriate lamp might be found was not confined to the mosques of Egypt. At the same time as he wrote to Cromer, Curzon asked the Imperial Library to send him any books they might have on Saracenic art. In particular, he suggested, 'the lavishly illustrated edition of the *Arabian Nights* which he used to pore over in his childhood' might have such designs. Alas, the Imperial Library had no copy of the *Arabian Nights*. In the end, on his way back to England at the end of his viceroyalty, Curzon stopped over in Cairo, where he himself visited the principal mosques and museums, and placed an order for a lamp made from an Arabic model. 'I trust', he wrote, after its installation, 'that the lamp may hang there as my last tribute to the glories of Agra which float like a vision of eternal beauty in my memory'.[18]

Perhaps Curzon's lamp might be taken to represent the colonial aesthetic. It is an aesthetic of difference, of distance, of subordination, of control—an aesthetic in which the Taj Mahal, the mosques of Cairo, even the *Arabian Nights*, all merge and become indistinguishable, and hence are available for use however the colonial ruler chooses. It is an aesthetic in which the past, though ordered with scrupulous attention to detail, stays firmly in the past. It is an aesthetic Shah Jahan could never have comprehended.

---

[1] Curzon to Cromer, 19 April 1905, in OIOC Curzon Papers, F111/621/p/173.

[2] T. Roger Smith, 'Architectural art in India', *Journal of the Society of Arts*, vol.21 (1873); *The Builder*, 10 September 1870, p.723. For further discussion see Thomas R. Metcalf, *An Imperial Vision: Indian architecture and Britain's Raj* (California, 1989), esp.ch.3.

[3] See Catherine B. Asher and Thomas R. Metcalf (eds.), *Perceptions of India's Visual Past* (New Delhi, 1994), esp.pp.8-10. For an earlier instance, see Joanna Williams, 'A recut Asokan capital and the Gupta attitude toward the past', *Artibus Asiae*, vol.35 (1973), pp.225-40.

[4] H.H. Cole, *Illustrations of Buildings near Muttra and Agra Showing the Mixed Hindu-Mohamedan Style of Upper India* (London, 1873).

[5] For instance, see Richard Davis, 'Indian art objects as loot', *Journal of Asian Studies*, vol.52 (1993), pp.22-48; and George Michell, 'Revivalism as an imperial mode', in Asher and Metcalf (eds.), *Perceptions of India's Visual Past*, pp.187-98.

[6] See Vishakha N. Desai, 'Reflections of India's past in the present: copying processes in Indian painting', in Asher and Metcalf (eds.), *Perceptions of India's Visual Past*, pp.135-48.

[7] See, for example, Benedict Anderson, *Imagined Communities* (London, 1990), ch.2; and David Lowenthal, *The Past is a Foreign Country* (1985).

[8] James Ransome, 'European architecture in India', *Journal of the Royal Institute of British Architects*, 3rd ser., vol.12 (1905), pp.185-203.

[9] Curzon Minutes of 11 May 1902, NAI For.Secret-I September 1902, no.1-3; and of 21 October 1902, NAI For.Intl-B November 1902, no.463-64. For a general discussion of British ritual see Bernard S. Cohn, 'Representing authority in Victorian India', in E. Hobsbawm and T. Ranger (ed.), *The Invention of Tradition* (Cambridge, 1983), pp.165-209.

[10] James Fergusson, 'On the study of Indian architecture', *Journal of the Society of Arts*, vol.15 (1866), pp.71-80; Curzon speech to Asiatic Society, Calcutta, 7 February 1900, in Thomas Raleigh (ed.), *Curzon in India* (London, 1906), pp.182-94. See also Metcalf, *An Imperial Vision*, ch.2, for a general account.

[11] Curzon speech of 7 February 1900, in Raleigh, *Curzon in India*, pp.182-94.

[12] See Narayani Gupta, *Delhi Between Two Empires* (Delhi, 1981); Norma Evenson, *The Indian Metropolis* (New Haven, 1989), esp.pp.99-104, 149-50; and Hosagrahr Jyoti, 'Urban Transformation as Cultural Politics: Negotiating Urbanism in Old Delhi', University of California, Berkeley, PhD dissertation (in progress).

[13] Gwendolyn Wright, *The Politics of Design in French Colonial Urbanism* (Chicago, 1991), esp.ch.3.

[14] C.E. Spooner, speech reported in *Selangor Journal*, vol.5, 2 April 1897, pp.238-9. For discussion of the building's design, see J.M. Gullick, 'The Bangunan Sultan Ahmad Samad', *Journal of the Malay Branch of the Royal Asiatic Society*, vol.65 (1992), pp.27–37.

[15] Jagmohan Mahajan, *The Raj Landscape: British view of Indian cities* (New Delhi, 1988), pp.138-45. See also Mildred Archer, *Early Views of India* (London, 1980), esp. plates 27-29.

[16] William Emerson, 'On the Taj Mahal at Agra', *Transactions of the Royal Institute of British Architects*, 1 ser., vol.20 (1869-70), pp.195-203.

[17] See, for instance, Curzon to Hamilton, 23 April 1902, Curzon to LaTouche, 28 January 1905, and further correspondence in Curzon Papers F111/621, pp.109, 136, 146 and passim.

[18] See Curzon to Imperial Library, 4 and 14 April 1905, to British Agency in Cairo, 27 July 1905, to Louis Dane, 24 June 1906, and to J.P. Hewett, 24 November 1908, in Curzon Papers F111/621.

Chapter Two

TALES OF THE BHARHUT STUPA: ARCHAEOLOGY IN THE COLONIAL AND NATIONALIST IMAGINATIONS[1]

Tapati Guha-Thakurta

This chapter has as its broad canvas the workings of archaeology in colonial India, both as a new field of authoritative knowledge on India's 'antiquities' (a category encompassing ruined monuments, architectural and sculptural fragments, inscriptions and coins), and as a new mode of historical imagination. It traces archaeology's self-formulation as a discipline over the late nineteenth century, the emerging textual and institutional contours of the field, and the manner in which it constituted its objects of study.[2] At the same time, it explores the way the disciplinary field opened up a terrain for the scholarly and popular imagination. The 'imagination', here, while claiming the legitimacy of scholarship, can often be seen to push beyond the boundaries of what could always be empirically known and attested. This raises certain crucial questions: how did a discipline like archaeology work within a local and national context? How was a 'Western' field of expertise and practice strategically transformed into an area of 'national' knowledge? In what ways were the same archaeological sites and structures made available as relics of a national past?

As a backdrop to these narratives, the chapter juxtaposes the emergence of a new specialised domain of Western scholarship in the late nineteenth century with the writings of the first Bengali antiquarians and archaeologists in the same field. The scholarly field, we find, emerged as an arena not just of participation, but also of contest and parallel claims. It would undergo subtle mutations as an indigenous intelligentsia staked its claims to equal knowledge and worked out separate subject positions within it. A kind of separate or parallel space within the field, that can be seen to emerge since the 1870s, assumed different dimensions over the turn of the century, as the scholarly cause tied up with the nationalist agenda of creating a popular regional forum in the recovery of the past. This reflected itself significantly in the dual location of these Bengali scholars, both within and outside the discipline, and in the bilingual scope of their work. It also brought on their periodic choice of a fictionalised narrative genre, that involved a continuous blending of the academic with the popular, of history with collective memory, of the exigencies of proof with those of persuasion.

The chapter brings these themes to bear around one key archaeological monument of ancient India, excavated in the 1870s—the Buddhist *stupa* at Bharhut in central India dated around the second century B.C.—and on two very different types of representation invoked around it in the writings of a British and a Bengali scholar. The Bharhut *stupa*, one of the most important 'discoveries' of the Archaeological Survey of India, provides us with a striking example of the way a single monument, located within a corpus of other structures and styles, could stand as a symbol of India's most glorious ancient past (the age of Asoka and early Buddhism) and the high point of the Indian art tradition (early Buddhist architecture and sculpture) (Fig. 1). The monument found its authoritative account in 1879 in a large, lavishly illustrated volume written by Alexander Cunningham, then the Director of the Archaeological Survey of India. Cunningham's book, a typical specimen of the genre of scholarship that held sway in the field, could be set up as a master text, with direct leads into other parallel documentation and display projects of this period, with resonances which carried over into the first comprehensive histories of Indian art and architecture produced in the same years.

During 1914-15, the Bharhut *stupa* featured again as the centrepiece within a newly-developed genre of historical fiction in Bengal. This 'historical romance', as it was designated, was written by Rakhaldas Banerjee, one of the foremost Bengali archaeologists who had successfully established himself within the new professional sphere. Rakhaldas Banerjee's *Pashaner Katha* (The tale of a stone slab), where a stone fragment of the Bharhut *stupa* narrates a story that becomes the microcosm of the nation's ancient history, positions us at an interesting nationalised space in the work of Bengali archaeologists and art historians. A separate space that had begun to emerge in the 1870s, through challenges to the viewpoint of Western scholars, assumed different dimensions with the turn of the century, as a new professional breed of Bengali archaeologists reached out to a wide local readership in building a sense of a regional and a national past. The chapter will explore these contiguous and contending spheres of representation, as new national/popular histories shaped themselves out of a legacy of modern knowledge.

The colonial project: mapping out Indian antiquities

The career and writings of Alexander Cunningham[3] (stretching from his first travels and investigations in the 1840s up to his retirement from the directorship of the Archaeological Survey of India in 1885) encapsulates a crucial transition in British approaches to Indian antiquities. It inaugurates a new colonial obsession with 'scientific', institutionalised knowledge on India's history and tradition. Cunningham's proposal of 1861 for a systematic archaeological investigation of Indian antiquities stirred the same concerns in Lord Canning, the Governor-General of India:

> It will not be to our credit as an enlightened ruling power if we continue to allow such fields of investigation, as the remains of the old Buddhist capital of Behar, the vast ruins of Kanouj, the plains around Delhi, studded with ruins more thickly than even the Campagna of Rome...to remain without more examination than they have hitherto received. Everything that has hitherto been done in this way has been done by private persons, imperfectly, and without system....[4]

What was seen as particularly important at this stage, was the replacement of scattered individual initiatives by a more systematised, centralised pattern of investigation, under governmental direction. The idea was also to demarcate a specialised sphere of 'archaeological investigation'—to enable field archaeology, with its interest in the excavation, identification and classification of sites, to be instituted as a separate discipline within, and out of a broader arena of, antiquarian studies. In 1861, the Government of India decided to establish the Archaeological Survey, and Cunningham began a new phase of study and exploration in his appointment as Archaeological Surveyor to the government.

Cunningham's career had an important parallel in that of another contemporary British scholar working in the same vast untapped field of Indian 'antiquities', James Fergusson. As the first scholar of a new subject he defined as 'Indian architecture', Fergusson marked a conscious departure from the earlier 'picturesque' approach to Indian antiquities to a new concern with accurate description and documentation of ancient monuments. Fergusson distinguished his own project from those of travelling European artists in India in the early nineteenth century, for whom India's ruins had featured as key ingredients in the composition of 'picturesque' sceneries. The sets of aquatints of William Hodges (made in the 1780s) and of Thomas and William Daniell (made over 1795-1808) were taken up primarily by the grandeur and desolation of ruined monuments set in rugged landscape.[5] Fergusson, by contrast, set about discovering forms and styles, systems and structures in these relics. When, as an indigo-planter in India, Fergusson went on his extensive travels across the country between 1835 and 1842, sketching, taking notes and documenting buildings with the help of a camera lucida, all was, in his own words 'darkness and uncertainty'. Functioning then as a kind of 'one-man architectural survey', he regretted that he had no account whatsoever of the art and architectural history of India to guide him, nor any criteria by which to judge the age and style of the buildings he encountered.[6] By the time Fergusson completed his work, publishing his comprehensive *History of Indian and Eastern Architecture* in 1876, a large number of Indian monuments had been surveyed, and a broad pattern and chronology of stylistic development established. Most important, Fergusson, it is widely acknowledged, had systematised the study of Indian architecture as a discipline in itself, converging variously on archaeology, ethnography and art history.[7]

One of Fergusson's earliest books that resulted from his study tours, *Picturesque Illustrations of Ancient Architecture in Hindostan* (1848), clearly laid out his intentions and methods. Despite its invocation of the 'picturesque', the work was premised on the accuracy and correctness of Fergusson's representations of Indian architecture vis-à-vis those of the Daniells; the twenty-four large lithographed plates were to be valued less as 'pleasing artistic compositions' and more as authentic sources of 'information and instruction'.[8] Information and instruction were the keynotes of Fergusson's entire scholarly project. Convinced of the intrinsic connection between knowledge and empire, between the British command over India's past and the command over her present destiny, Fergusson was equally convinced that proper knowledge of India's history could only stem from as close, as careful and as exhaustive a survey of her ancient monuments as he had done. What followed in Fergusson was an increasing reliance on pure architectural evidence (of structure and style) in identifying buildings and according them a history. What also emanated from such a method was his own sense of authority and uniqueness within his field—a feeling of mastery that came from the notion that there were none to rival the intimacy and thoroughness of his acquaintance with the objects of study.

While such a stance would later culminate in extreme egoism, it produced, during the 1860s, Fergusson's powerful plea for the study of Indian architecture 'on its own terms'. In his manifesto on the subject in 1867,[9] he highlighted the major aesthetic and intellectual compulsions for such a study. One compulsion lay in the vital lessons of a continuous living tradition, as against the artificial revival of dead 'classical' styles; the lessons of superior principles of ornamental design as against the 'vulgar' illusionist style that had permeated contemporary Western design; the lessons also of a truly natural and organic production, where forms, function and material were in harmony and the ornaments grew naturally out of the structures. Another compulsion lay in the advancement of Western knowledge about Indian civilisation, in the elucidation of the ancient history, religions, customs and ethnography of the Indian people. While it epitomised the 'true' and 'higher' principles of architectural form, Indian antiquities carried the other supreme value of historical evidence. Compared to languages or literatures, architecture was seen as a far more reliable index of the past—'…it never shifts its locality, and…it does not change with time; and…we know exactly what the religion, what the art and the civilisation of the people were who excavated [the structures]'.[10] If the architecture of India was indeed to be read as a 'great stone book, in which each tribe and race has written its annals and recorded its faith',[11] then the ground needed to be prepared by an extensive programme of documentation (through drawings, photographs, copies and casts) of all architectural specimens. For Fergusson, in particular, with his reliance on pure architectural evidence, the precision and accuracy of illustration was a major issue at stake (and a main point of attack against others working in the field). It was largely on the strength of a memorandum he submitted to the government in 1868, urging the preparation and acquisition of casts and copies of all old Indian architectural and sculptural remains for museums in England, that the illustration and collection of Indian art entered a new, organised phase.[12]

An Archaeological Survey report of 1869, on 'the illustration of the Archaic Architecture of India', contained a long listing by Fergusson of all the 'architectural objects' in India of which photographs and casts were to be obtained, with a line-up of monuments and remains, region by region in each of the Presidencies.[13] The aim was towards a thorough and representative selection that could effectively embody the subject of India's art and architectural history. The esoteric subject of 'Indian antiquities' was now being processed into a system of regional, chronological and religious classifications, that would soon find a fuller elaboration in Fergusson's comprehensive *History*. And an overlapping of 'age-value', 'historical value' and 'aesthetic value'[14] determined the selection and incorporation of antiquities within the new archaeological scheme of documentation and conservation. The same report also contained Alexander Cunningham's general grouping of all 'the archaeological remains of India' under the four heads of architecture, sculpture, coins and inscriptions, providing in each case a detailed break-up and dating under categories like early Buddhist, later Buddhist, Indo-Scythian, Jain, early Brahmanical, later Brahmanical, early and later Muhammadan.[15]

Cunningham's memorandum underlined the main difference in his interests and methods from those of Fergusson. Whereas the latter worked solely with the stylistic and structural evidence of monuments, Cunningham emphasised the greater authority of inscriptions or coins in ascertaining the dates and dynastic links of buildings, and the importance of his own expertise in ancient Indian epigraphy and numismatics. As he launched on a new phase of explorations as Archaeological Surveyor to the government in the 1860s, Cunningham was concerned both with locating himself within a distinguished lineage of Western initiatives in the field, and with sifting out the distinctness of his own enterprise.[16]

In the history of the study of Indian antiquities that Cunningham presented, Prinsep's decipherment of the ancient Brahmi and Kharoshti scripts and the Arian Pali alphabets in 1834 was singled out as a momentous break-through. It opened up a vast new arena of investigation in Bactrian-Greek coins, in Sanskrit and Pali legends in coins, and in the Asokan pillar edicts. The age of the first 'Closet or Scholastic Archaeologists' (men like William Jones, H.T. Colebrooke or H.H. Wilson) gave way to that of 'field archaeologists' and 'travelling antiquarians' like Cunningham.[17] The search for India's ancient history shifted premises from classical texts to coins, epigraphs and archaeological sites. Employed as Assay Master of the Calcutta Mint, Prinsep, between 1834 and 1838, had plunged himself fully into his alternative vocation of deciphering coins and edicts, even as the young Cunningham was branching from a career as military surveyor and engineer into the excavation of antiquarian remains. Cunningham's scholarly self-positioning rested on a strong sense of partnership with Prinsep, and of a shared mission of discoveries.[18] He placed himself in a line with several others (among them James Fergusson) who followed up Prinsep's work in the next three decades (1840s, '50s and '60s), surveying and interpreting antiquities in different regions.

At the same time, Cunningham in this period strongly pressed for the substitution of scattered individual initiatives for systematic government-sponsored survey, which he, in his wide experience and travels, would be best equipped to lead. He, more than anyone else, now advanced the agenda for an organised countrywide investigation and preservation of ancient monuments. In the course of his surveys the new discipline of field-archaeology established itself, out of the grounds prepared by numismatics, epigraphy and architectural studies. Spanning the entire sweep of upper India from the hills of the north-western frontier to lower Bengal, the plains of Malwa and Chattisgarh and the uplands of Mahakosala and Bundelkhand, what Cunningham's surveys also did was to 'map out' a definition of ancient India in the topography of her archaeological sites.[19] Side by side with colonial cartography, colonial archaeology began to 'map out' ancient India in a new landscape of ruins.

In search of the Buddhist past

The historical geography of ancient India which Cunningham laid out through his surveys had a decidedly Buddhist focus. For Cunningham, it must be remembered, was not undertaking the exploration of the modern mapped-out territory of British India. What he indulged in, rather, was a select refiguring of ancient India in a period set up as the high point of her history and civilisation. His archaeological explorations sought largely to retrace the steps and travel itinerary of the ancient Buddhist pilgrims from China, Fa Hsien and Hiuen Tsang.[20] Where classical sources such as Pliny's and Ptolemy's geographies had been the main aid for early pioneers of Indian cartography like James Rennell, Stanislas Julien's translation of Hiuen Tsang's travels provided new explorers with an exciting new source. Where Pliny in his Eastern Geography had followed the route of Alexander's invasion, the archaeologist could now follow in the footsteps of Hiuen Tsang, attempting at each stage to relate the Chinese versions of place names to corresponding Sanskrit ones, and thereafter to relate the Sanskrit names to the sites and monuments excavated.[21] This is what Cunningham set out to do in his surveys, retrieving the ancient geography and history of India primarily in terms of Buddhist sites.

Much of the investigation of Indian antiquities in this period (1830-1860) had, in any case, been weighted towards Buddhist remains and their leads into the Indo-Greek connections of the north-west. Prinsep had been the first to identify correctly the large number of 'topes' or *stupas* being opened up in the north-west with Buddhist religious structures. Alongside, an increasing interest in the Indo-Greek coins and sculptures being unearthed from this region had led to the enthused discovery of the Gandhara school of Buddhist sculpture of this area, with their marked Graeco-Roman influences. The Gandhara sculptures offered the Western scholar a sample of an Indian art form which, in its identifiable link with classical Hellenic art, could be accommodated within the established European canon of artistic excellence.[22] What was seen to be remarkable about these Gandhara sculptures, however, was not just their affinity to the Greek ideal, but also 'their decided Buddhist character', their original location within Buddhist religious edifices of which they were part and parcel. Just as the excellence of Hellenic art was associated with the greatness of the civilisation of Periclean Athens, the 'superior' qualities which the British perceived in Buddhist art came to hinge on a broader construct of the 'purity' of Buddhist religion and culture in India.

One of Buddhism's major values for the nineteenth-century British scholar was as an antithesis to the 'degenerate' Brahmanical religion they confronted in both India's past and present. There was a clear polemical and political edge to the antiquarian fascination with India's Buddhist past. Cunningham, for instance, had brought home the 'greater' benefits involved in his project of searching out the Buddhist ruins of India. By exposing its flaws and underplaying the importance of Brahmanism as *the* paramount religion of India, he felt that the vision of a counter religious system of the past could assist in the present-day propagation of Christianity in the country. He also believed that Buddhism underlined the lesson that India was politically strong and resistant to external invasions only when united under one ruler, as she was once again under the British empire.[23]

But, soon purged of such overt imperial motivations, the obsession with the Buddhist past continued, constructing it as the essence and peak of India's ancient history. For Fergusson, India's architectural history 'began' with Buddhism and with its high tide under the reign of King Asoka (c.268-266 B.C.).[24] The early phase of Buddhist architecture and sculpture provided for him (and for many others in the field), an apex in a theory of the 'inverted evolution' of Indian art; it exemplified the point of excellence from which the history of Indian art and religion moved from 'purity' to 'corruptions', from 'rational' order and simplicity to 'degenerate' idolatry, iconography and excess of ornamentation.[25]

Cunningham's archaeological investigations also proceeded within much the same framework. However, the dominant paradigm for his work was not that of artistic progress and decline, but that of emphasising the greater value of antiquities over religious texts as sources for India's ancient history. It is in him that we can clearly see the major epistemic shift that was occurring over this period in Western strategies for unlocking the mysteries of India's past—the shift from philology to archaeology as the new authenticating ground for Indian history. The Buddhist antiquities that had been uncovered, he believed, spoke far more eloquently and authentically about India's past than 'all the rubbish contained in the 18 Puranas' (texts which were completely silent about Buddhism), with the clearly implied connotation that the history which Buddhist remains revealed was also the more worthy and grander sample of ancient Indian civilisation.[26] Consequently, all three of Cunningham's detailed archaeological monographs would centre around early Buddhist sites: around the *stupas* of Sanchi, Bharhut and Bodhgaya.

Earlier, in 1843, one of his first discoveries of Buddhist ruins—the ancient city of Sankisa in the United Provinces—had laid out what would become the standard features of a Cunningham report: a ground survey of the height and extent of the mounds; a lay-out of the structural features and measurements of the architectural remains; a record of their local traditions; a search for references to the place in ancient literary texts and in Chinese travel accounts; an identification of the sacred places and monuments mentioned in the latter with various surviving features on the ground; finally, a mention of the coins, inscriptions and other remains recovered from the vicinity and the corroborative information they supplied.[27] Cunningham's first major book of 1852 on the Sanchi *stupa* (surveying five groups of *stupas* in the Bhilsa region of central India) offered a full elaboration of this method.[28] It brought together all the substantive details of field-excavations with an analysis of the data, a careful and complete description of the monument with elaborate drawings of the ground-plans and sculpted reliefs.

The work established a new genre of lavish archaeological publications. It also focused attention on a monument (and a corresponding group) that would be at the centre of the colonial programmes of documentation and conservation. The Sanchi *stupa* (dated between the first century B.C. and A.D.), as a prime example of early Buddhist architecture with a wealth of sculptures, became the subject of further detailed sets of drawings, photographs and conservation programmes.[29] Alongside, as another Buddhist *stupa* at Amaravati (in the Guntur district of the Madras Presidency) came to light,[30] through excavations, drawings and photographs, there emerged the notion of a 'school' or a chain of Buddhist monuments, with the Sanchi *stupa* representing the early achievement of the Maurya and post-Maurya period and Amaravati the later development of the Gupta period. Between them, Sanchi and Amaravati came to stand in for the two 'golden ages' of ancient imperial India, containing within and between them the heyday of India's Buddhist civilisation. Illustrations of the Sanchi and Amaravati sculptures featured prominently in the collection of photographs of Indian architecture which Fergusson arranged for the Paris International Exhibition of 1867. Simultaneously, Fergusson launched another major project of retrieving history from these monuments, using the sculpted panels of Sanchi and Amaravati as a 'source' for studying the ethnography, mythology, customs and practices of this period.[31] So, for Fergusson, the facial features of sculpted figures served to illustrate the mix of Aryan and non-Aryan races in the population; while the representation of rituals and ceremonies in the friezes were seen to imply relative progressions from greater asceticism to greater sensual pleasures within the faith.

The stupa *of Bharhut*

These different projective currents surrounding the study of Buddhist antiquities provides the trajectory for Alexander Cunningham's next large monograph of 1879 on *The Stupa of Bharhut*: a work I have taken as an exemplar of colonial archaeology and its scholarly canon.[32] Following Hiuen Tsang's itinerary from the major Buddhist sites in Bihar (Gaya-Rajgir-Nalanda-Sarnath) up through the eastern United Provinces to Delhi, on to the major cluster of sites in the north-west (among them Taxila and Manikyala) and downwards to west and central India, Cunningham discovered the Bharhut *stupa* during a tour of the Baghelkhand region in 1873-4. Between the spring of 1874 and the summer of 1876, under Cunningham and his assistant, J.D. Beglar, the ruins were systematically explored, excavated and documented, recovering stones from a large surrounding area to reassemble the original structure as far as possible. The Bharhut *stupa* now came to stand most prominently among the ancient sites to be 'disinterred, unjungled, measured, photographed, reconstructed, fenced off, analysed and displayed'.[33] It was endowed with the unique singularity that would mark the most 'ancient' and 'monumental' of such sites, even as it found its place within a sequence of architectural styles and historical epochs. Dated between 200 and 150 B.C. and attributed to Buddhist kings of the Sunga dynasty of this region, the Bharhut *stupa* became a significant addition in the Sanchi-Amaravati chain of excellence of Buddhist art. It pushed the chain back in time beyond Sanchi to a moment of higher antiquity and superior achievement, initiating a privileged line of artistic development in ancient India. Its splendour of sculptures powerfully complemented the panels and pillars of Sanchi and Amaravati as 'illustrations' of Buddhist life, legend and history. 'Taking it all in all…and certainly in a historical point of view', the Bharhut *stupa* was marked out in Fergusson's new *History* as the most remarkable of ancient Indian monuments.[34]

Fig 1. Bharhut stupa: torana (OIOC; British Library)

Cunningham's text of 1879 exemplifies, more than anything else, the workings of this 'historical point of view' in the archaeological reconstruction of Bharhut. In later histories of Indian art and architecture, the Bharhut sculptures, along with those of Sanchi and Amaravati and the Buddha images of Mathura and Sarnath, would merit a more pointed 'artistic' evaluation, in contrast to this earlier phase of 'archaeological' restitution and documentation.[35] But in the 1870s, Cunningham's work on this monument typified the way archaeological practice constituted its 'regime of truth'; it typified its urge to measure, classify, label, restore and render a site viewable as a relic of 'history'.[36]

We can identify in this book all the main methods (some of them quite distinctive of Cunningham) of such 'historical' investigations of colonial archaeology. The initial chapter is taken up with locating Bharhut within 'the ancient geography of India' of the Buddhist period, searching out its references in Buddhist legend, tracing its history from its mention in Ptolemy's map and Hiuen Tsang's travels, through its incorporation within the dominions of the Gupta kings, and later of Harshavardhana, to its reduction to the rule of petty chieftains in the early medieval period. With 'the final blow' of the Muhammadan invasion, Bharhut disappears from history—from the gaze of the historian's searching eye—until the science of modern archaeology retrieves and restores 'true history' to the site.[37]

The historicising of the site relied centrally on the exercise of the correct dating of the *stupa*. Here Cunningham's epigraphic expertise is brought into play in the emphasis he lays on reading the large number of inscriptions available—inscriptions of royal donors financing the construction of the four magnificent gateways (*toranas*)—and in the 'absolute identity' he discerned between the characters of these inscriptions and those of the Asokan edicts and of coinage excavated in the vicinity.[38] These provided the main evidence for dating the *stupa* to a period between 200 and 150 B.C. and associating it with the reign of King Dhanabhuti I of the Sunga dynasty. The epigraphic evidence found corroboration in the stylistic evidence offered by Bharhut's sculpture and architectural ornamentation which seemed to stand half-way between those of the rail of Buddha Gaya (attributed to the Asokan period, that is, the third century B.C.) and those of the Sanchi gateways (dated at least a century or more later than the Bharhut *stupa*).

Historically positioned in space and time, the excavated *stupa* was then exposed, little by little, to a thorough scrutiny of description. The physical process of digging, clearing, identifying and piecing together fragments was replicated in the text's reconstruction of the entire architectural plan of the monument, as it must have 'originally stood'— the ground plan and elevation of the *stupa*, its height and width, location of each gateway and of each beam, pillar and railing within it, the location also of the continuous sculpted architrave threading together an inner and outer circle of pillars.[39] Following this overview of the entire structure, the largest section of the text was concerned with an exhaustive description of the sculptures, through a thematic classification. Fergusson, in his book on the Sanchi and Amaravati sculptures, had provided mainly an 'ethnographic' analysis, reconstructing from them a social history of the religion, customs, ritual practices and racial characteristics of the people they represented. Cunningham's treatment of the Bharhut sculptures, by contrast, was geared more to the illustration of 'Buddhist legend and history', working closely with Western manuals on Buddhist religion and mythology and with translations of old literary texts.[40] Thus, in meticulous detail, each sculpted scene would be identified with a tale in the Buddhist *Jatakas* or with an 'actual' event in Buddhist history, such as the construction of the Jetavana monastery, or the visit of Prince Ajatashatru to Buddha; the special Buddhist religious symbols (like the wheel, the footprints or the Bodhi tree), the different types of Buddhist buildings (like the *stupas*, *dharma chakras* or *vajrasanas*), or various superhuman mythic figures (like *Yakshas*, *Yakshinis*, *Devas* and *Nagas*) would be picked out in the sculptures. The exercise laid the groundwork for the kind of in-depth iconographic analysis that would become the dominant mode of scholarship in Indian art history. At the time the book was written, however, such a study contributed more directly to the colonial reification of India's Buddhist past. It reinforced the image of a lost 'purity' of faith, values and artistic form, before the downward slide to idolatry and other 'corrupt' practices,[41] of an 'ideal' ancient past from which Indians had been completely severed.

This theme of an insulated distant past, to be sifted out of all the decay and degeneration of present-day India, lay at the heart of the entire archaeological programme. It offered the conceptual paradigm in which a monument could be fully detached from the immediate reality of its people and environment, and transformed into a sacred archaeological relic: a purified repository of an 'original' past. The Bharhut *stupa* provides us with a powerful case. For the very story of its archaeological reconstruction is premised on the scenario of the ruin and demolition of the monument—of complete native ignorance about this ancient relic, and of the continuous pilfering of its stones by local

people for building purposes.[42] Native apathy and vandalism have as
their redemptive contrast the arduous archaeological project of clearing,
excavating and retrieving stones from all around to reassemble as far as
possible the 'original' structure and to preserve it as such. Thus, the
archaeological exercise also becomes a 'museumising' process.
Cunningham's text seems to fulfil the same purpose, which the
archaeological survey achieved. In its sheer volume of detail and
description, it renders the reconstructed monument into a state of 'total
surveyability';[43] as in a museum, every pillar and railing and each piece
of sculpture appears laid out for display and scholarly scrutiny.

Such a process is stretched to its ultimate in the case of the Bharhut
stupa. Recovered and restored, the monument, it was felt, could be
preserved from the local people only by its removal from the site and
its transference to the premises of a museum.[44] This radically
completed the process of its detachment and metamorphosis into a
piece of 'antiquity' and 'art'. That the Bharhut sculptures found their
way into the Indian Museum in Calcutta, rather than to the museum of
the India Office in London (as was hoped by some) was a reflection of
a particular thrust within colonial archaeology. The India that was being
unearthed in her archaeological sites was seen itself as a natural
museum: one of the world's oldest and largest. And a main concern
behind the schemes for a systematic illustration of all the best samples
of ancient Indian architecture and sculpture was that of preserving the
remains *in situ*, as much as possible, while supplying museums in India
and England with faithful copies (plaster casts, facsimiles, photographs
and drawings). The point was made clear by the Curator of Ancient
Monuments in India, a new post and department created in 1880:

> ...We are not answerable for keeping the Grecian marbles [in the British
> Museum]...; neither were we concerned for the rights of Egypt when
> Cleopatra's Needle left Alexandria for the Thames embankment. In the
> case, however, of India—a country which is a British possession—the
> arguments are different. We are, I submit, responsible for Indian
> monuments and for their preservation, *in situ*, when possible.[45]

In invoking this principle of higher 'responsibility', the British had
established their authority as saviours and custodians of India's
forgotten past. It was in the interest of preservation and safe
custodianship that the Bharhut *stupa* was made an exception (to the
rule) and removed in its entirety to the new archaeological galleries of
the Indian Museum in Calcutta.

By the time of the installation of the Bharhut sculptures in the Indian
Museum and the publication of Cunningham's book, the colonial

archaeological project had taken on its full modernised and energised form. Alongside regular explorations and surveys, spanning an expanding terrain, and the publication of annual reports and large lavish monographs, museum collections and displays had also become a part of the Archaeological Survey's programme. The transference of the entire collection of antiquities from the Asiatic Society of Bengal to a newly-separated entity of the Indian Museum in the 1860s, underlined the new role of museums. The Indian Museum in Calcutta came to stand henceforth as the nucleus of the various new fields of colonial knowledge, linked to all the major Survey departments: the Archaeological, the Anthropological, the Geological, and so on. From being a wonder-house of curiosities and antiquities, it became a nodal point for 'scientific', disciplinary specialisation.[46]

With a special archaeological nucleus formed within the Indian Museum outside the spectrum of ethnological, zoological or Natural History collections, the Bharhut *stupa* came to stand as one of the prime exhibits of this section. Cunningham's book served as the authoritative reference for the museum display, the aura of the object deeply entwined with the expertise of the text that elucidated it.[47] The Bharhut *stupa*, along with fragments of pillars and sculptures from Bodhgaya and some casts of the rock-cut temples of Orissa, formed the central 'Asoka Gallery'. This was complemented, in importance, by a large collection of Gandhara sculptures (along with other antiquities of the first to third centuries A.D.) in what was called the 'Indo-Scythian Gallery', and a still larger collection of Buddhist sculptures and friezes in a designated 'Gupta Gallery'; and the rest of the collection was classified loosely as 'Brahmanical', 'Jain' and 'Muhammadan' antiquities in a clearly receding order of priorities.

Indian history had been stamped with the theory of a 'golden' Buddhist age, blocked out into a few ancient great imperial epochs. This would remain a reigning image, continuously developed and buttressed by an expanding colonial establishment, even as a widening range of 'antiquities' from different periods and regions came under its purview, even as the subject of enquiry would later be transformed from 'antiquities' to 'art' in the hands of a new group of scholars. It is also this dominant image of the nation's antiquity and ancient glories which a new Indian intelligentsia appropriated, as they came to participate in the same modernised scholarly field.

Indigenous interventions: 'The problem with native knowledge'

From its inception, the colonial archaeological project had counted on the involvement of Indians—a new group of 'trained', 'educated' Indians, converted to their cause of scholarly investigations. It had been the government's express desire in 1870 that 'as far as possible intelligent "natives" should be employed in, and trained to, the task of photography, measuring and surveying buildings, directing excavations and...deciphering inscriptions'.[48] The most eminent of such 'intelligent natives' who entered the field in this period was Rajendralal Mitra (1822-91), by then an established antiquarian and Indologist and an important member of the Asiatic Society of Bengal. He came to head one of the most extensive documentation and survey projects that the government had got under way since the late 1860s. Taking up a scheme floated by the Royal Society of Arts, London, for obtaining casts of old Indian sculpture, Rajendralal Mitra turned to the ancient temple architecture and sculpture of Orissa, taking with him on his study tours a team of student artists of the Calcutta School of Art. The end product of this project, Rajendralal Mitra's two-volume book, *The Antiquities of Orissa* (1875-80), along with his work on the Buddhist monastery of *Buddha Gaya* (1878), stood in line with the Western publications on Indian archaeology, with the same objectives, the same details of description and classification, and the same abundance of illustrative plates.[49] They fitted fully into the new academic genre, internalising the scientificity of its methods and intentions.

However, Rajendralal Mitra's work also turns our attention to a parallel site of nationalist claims and aspirations that emerged within the same terrain. It shows how Western knowledge, used on its own rigorous terms of proof and argument, could become an instrument for asserting the antiquity and autonomy of the Indian art tradition. In many ways, Rajendralal Mitra's work seemed to take its cue directly from Fergusson's: it shared the same concerns with accuracy and detail, with the 'educational' value of ancient Indian architectural design as models for study and copying in the art schools, or, for instance, with the 'historical value' of the Orissa temple sculptures as an index to the ethnography, religion, custom and social usages of the period. Yet, using the same props and methods, Rajendralal Mitra would labour his points of difference with Fergusson. For Fergusson, the excess of decoration in Hindu architecture was a sure sign of its 'decadence'; for Rajendralal, on the contrary, the 'grandeur' of ornamentation in Orissan temple architecture became the definitive mark of its 'fine art' status, and the precision and intricacy of the student's drawings in his book, he believed, amply supported this counter-case.[50] Then again, his ethnographic analyses of the Bhubaneswar temple sculptures, resisting Fergusson's views of racial mixing and hybridisation, were intended to establish the 'Aryan' pedigree of the sculpted figures, to mark out a 'national Indo-Aryan' type in facial features, physiognomy and style of dress.[51]

Most important of all was Rajendralal's refutation of Fergusson's opinion about the non-existence of stone architecture in India prior to the age of Asoka and the period of contact with the Bactrian Greeks, and his theory of the replication of prior wooden models in the first stone buildings in India of the second and first centuries B.C. For Rajendralal the very maturity and finish of the Asokan stone pillars, and of the sculpted friezes and architecture of the Orissa cave temples of a near-contemporary period stood as 'positive proof' of a long pre-existing and autonomous tradition of building and sculpting in stone in ancient India. To argue a case from the mere absence of stone remains of an anterior period (as Fergusson had done) was, in his view, a conversion of 'the negation of proof into a positive proof'. The carry-over of styles and structures in Orissa temples, he argued, was not from earlier wooden models, nor even from Greek buildings, but from the 'non-Aryan Tamilian' architectural traditions of southern India.[52] Thus, claiming all the while a similar reliance on 'architectural evidence' and a similar fidelity to proof, Rajendralal sought to 'correct' the history which Fergusson had imported to Indian architecture.

On the face of it, it was an academic quarrel over the perennially-contested themes of 'origin' and 'influence' in art history. But for both contestants, there were clearly larger issues at stake. Rajendralal Mitra's arguments were shot through with nationalist claims about the *antiquity, autonomy* and complete *originality* of the architectural tradition of ancient India, of which he identified some of the finest and 'purest' specimens in the Orissa temples.[53] Fergusson's response, while it clarified his unchanged views on the subject and Rajendralal Mitra's misconceptions of his standpoint, more overtly politicised the debate.[54] Straying far from the academic terrain of proof and evidence, Fergusson's self-defence against Rajendralal Mitra exploded into a general statement of colonial insecurity and consternation concerning Western-educated Indians (particularly about the 'vilest' specimen of these: the Bengali *babu*). The context was the highly charged political atmosphere surrounding the Ilbert Bill, a bill that threatened to subject the British in India to the jurisdiction of native judges; and what was being called into question was the very capacity of Indians for neutral unprejudiced 'knowledge'.[55] Fergusson set up Rajendralal Mitra as a prototype of native conceit, insubordination, ingratitude and faulty assimilation of Western learning.

His attack brings to the surface the chief undercurrent of tension— the tussle over scholarly domains. The subject was ultimately Fergusson's; the power to represent and authenticate India's past was ultimately a Western prerogative. Rajendralal Mitra was faulted for his 'superficial familiarity' with the subject, for his lack of 'knowledge of architectural draftsmanship, surveying or plan drawing even to a limited degree'.[56] A particular field of expertise was thus laid out to include some and pointedly exclude others: by the same criteria, later histories of Indian archaeology would classify Rajendralal Mitra more as an 'antiquarian' than an 'archaeologist in the modern sense'.[57] For Fergusson, though, the problem was not just with Rajendralal Mitra but with 'native knowledge' in general: a knowledge that was invariably based on 'memory' rather than on 'reason' and 'scientific training' and thus 'sadly wanting in depth and earnestness'. The critical point here then, was the contrast between Western and native learning—between the 'long study and careful reasoning' through which the former 'assimilated the great truths of scientific knowledge', and the superficiality, conceit, and memorising traits of the latter.[58]

Resolving and exploring 'difference'

Such invocations of difference (difference both in the form and content of learning) can be seen to contain vital potentials of inversion, opening up multiple possibilities for nationalism in subsequent years. They provide leads into a number of ways in which new genres of indigenous writing and scholarship in Bengal would appropriate the subject, redefine it, or mark out their autonomous stand and space within it. At one level we can see a distinct closing of the 'gap' between Western and Indian scholarship within the established academic discipline with the emergence of a growing body of Indian professional archaeologists. At another level we witness a powerful and polemical orchestration of difference, a reversal of the relative values attached to the 'Western' and 'Indian' points of view on the subject within a new body of Orientalist and nationalist writing. As the field itself was sharply split between an 'archaeological' and an 'artistic' approach, the subject of Indian art was removed from the sphere of antiquarian or archaeological expertise to one of 'aesthetic' and 'spiritual' empathy; and the importance of reason and scientific knowledge came to be challenged by the counter-values of intuition, idealism and artistic sensibility. The 'Indian' became synonymous with an 'aesthetic'/'idealistic' point of view. Thus construed as a superior order and celebrated for its sheer difference from earlier 'Western' orders of knowledge, it came to be cultivated by both European and Indian scholars in the hope of a more authentic appraisal of the national art tradition.[59]

At yet another level, we can trace both a resolution and exploration of 'difference' between the colonial and nationalist projects of recovering the past. We see this in the way a new group of professional historians and archaeologists, while working within the paradigms set by Western scholarship, evolved a parallel separate sphere of work in Bengali. As they diversified into a new linguistic and narrative genre, their 'modern' expertise and methods needed blending with a 'traditional' fund of collective memory and belief. Their academic project of archaeology or ancient history required new forms of popular authentication to gain credence with a national historical imagination. Moving to the first decades of the twentieth century, we will now be turning to this third level of indigenous writing in Bengali, taking up the case of Rakhaldas Banerjee (1886-1930) and the historical tale he wrote in Bengali around the archaeological relic we have already encountered—the *stupa* of Bharhut.

Rakhaldas Banerjee, however, needs to be situated against the vast transformation of approach and interest that had overtaken the subject of Indian art history. A subject that had so long featured merely within a 'dry' scheme of ordering, classifying or conserving, and marginalised within a Eurocentric canon of artistic excellence, was now being accorded its proper 'aesthetic' value, and located within an alternative zone of 'Indian' idealism and spirituality. At the same time, the state archaeological apparatus underwent much elaboration and centralisation under the Viceroy, Lord Curzon, and the new director-general, John Marshall. Curzon, as the self-proclaimed protector of Indian antiquities, set out the cornerstones of the 'scientific scheme' of Indian archaeology—'...it is equally our duty to dig and discover, to classify, reproduce and describe, to copy and decipher, and to cherish and conserve'.[60] But it was precisely in this definition of its own scope that the field of archaeological scholarship could be set aside by a new Orientalist lobby, which saw itself as the 'true' saviours of Indian art and tradition. By 1910, Cunningham and Fergusson had been superseded by two other powerful figures, E.B. Havell and A.K.

Coomaraswamy as the new authorities on a subject they recast from 'Indian antiquities' to 'Indian art and aesthetics'.

In consciously positioning itself outside official art administration in India, this new Orientalism struck up a close alliance with the nationalist art movement in Bengal led by Abanindranath Tagore.[61] The same opposition between the 'archaeological' and the 'aesthetic' standpoint came to be replayed, with different resonances, within the nationalist discourses on art history and aesthetics in Bengal. And similar claims to an exclusive 'aesthetic' and 'Indian' disposition gave Abanindranath Tagore's art movement (as it gave Havell and Coomaraswamy) its unique position of authority and unique nationalist self-image. The power of the new Orientalist lobby was replicated in the way this art movement established its nationalist hegemony: its claims to speak for all of Indian art and all of Indian nationalism.

This context stamped a particular meaning and connotation to Rakhaldas Banerjee's position as an archaeologist, working on the same artefacts of Indian art in the same years. One of my main interests here lies in retrieving the work of such Bengali archaeologists from this sphere into which it was cast—to relocate it in the interstices of a dominant 'colonial' and 'nationalist' programme, and look at the way it contributed equally to the shaping of a sense of a regional and national past in Bengal.

Initially, the divide between an 'archaeological' and an 'aesthetic' approach was orchestrated less around Rakhaldas Banerjee and more around another contemporary archaeologist and historian, Akshay Kumar Maitreya (1861-1930). In a lively debate carried out in Bengali journals through the second decade of the twentieth century, Akshay Maitreya challenged what he saw to be the 'transgression and distortion' of traditional aesthetic canons in Abanindranath Tagore's new school of 'Indian' painting. Abanindranath's 'aesthetic' reconstruction of Indian art came to be attacked for its 'lack of history and scholarship'; his privileging of artistic licence and imagination came to be countered by Maitreya's repeated recourse to historical proof and evidence. This debate remains outside the scope of this paper. None the less, I introduce Akshay Maitreya here because he most significantly sets out the paradigm (both the 'archaeological' and the 'local'/'popular' paradigm) within which we can place the parallel work of Rakhaldas Banerjee.

At the turn of the century, Akshay Maitreya stood at the head of a wave of independent indigenous initiatives in history and archaeology that delved primarily into the ancient and medieval past of Bengal. His

work points to the 'regional' and 'local' tropes that had come into play
within nationalist constructions of a composite 'Indian' past. A
developed regional cultural identity of the Bengalis now claimed both a
synonymity with and a special place within the image of the nation; it
chose, for instance, for the art of ancient *Gauda* (with *Gauda* clearly
prefiguring modern Bengal) a privileged role at the origin of the
development of a national and a greater Indian art tradition that would
encompass even the island of Java in the eighth and ninth centuries.[62]
Akshay Maitreya, in his Bengali historical novels,[63] in one of the first
Bengali historical journals he began in 1899-1900,[64] and in the local
archaeological research unit he established at Rajshahi in 1910, would
eminently carry through the project of conjuring up a Bengali national
past.

The project had its marked popular and nationalist overtones. With a
central objective of recovering Bengal's 'true' and 'glorious' history
from colonial misrepresentations, it retrieved for popular imagination
the much maligned figures of the last Muslim Nawabs as the last of
Bengal's 'independent' kings, also discovering in parallel many
forgotten Hindu heroes in Bengal's medieval history. The popular
project was, however, mediated by a rigorous academic one, with
Akshay Maitreya (as historian and archaeologist) repeatedly
underlining his commitment to 'evidence' and 'fact', and the need to
inculcate modern historical sense in his milieu. This is where he
authorised archaeology as a main field of scientific knowledge.
Emphasising his own expertise in it, he also pressed the importance of
opening up the field to a wider public, of popularising in Bengali its
main tenets of method and practice.[65] In reaction against the dominant
nationalist discourse in Indian art, we find Akshay Maitreya carving out
a counter-sphere of legitimacy for the archaeologist, according him the
privileged 'right' to represent the past and the special 'duty' of
retrieving for the nation its true authenticated history. Rakhaldas
Banerjee's work, belonging to the same period, finds its place within
this relegitimised, nationalised sphere of archaeology in Bengal.

Rakhaldas epitomised the new breed of professional Indian
archaeologists of the Curzon era, employed in government service and
directly sustaining its programmes. As a college student with a passion
for archaeology and ancient history, he studied Sanskrit with the
renowned Bengali *pandit*, Haraprasad Shastri, and epigraphy and
paleography with Theodore Bloch, then superintendent of the
Archaeological section of the Indian Museum in Calcutta. He soon
developed a wide-ranging expertise in epigraphy, numismatics, field

excavations and art history—in all the main domains that constituted the 'field' of ancient Indian history and archaeology. From his initial job in the Archaeological Department of the Indian Museum (1910-11), he moved to the Archaeological Survey of India, and in 1917 became the Superintendent of its Western circle. In the subsequent years, Rakhaldas Banerjee's scholarship in English would range over a wide spectrum: from his first palaeographic study on *The Origins of the Bengali Script* (1919), to a set of general histories (based primarily on archaeological evidence) on *Prehistoric, Ancient and Hindu India*, the Indo-Scythian period, the imperial Gupta age and the Palas of Bengal,[66] to detailed archaeological monographs around single sites. The high point of his career came with his celebrated discovery of the ancient city of Mohenjodaro in the Indus Valley, in the excavations he carried out over 1921-2: an archaeological *tour de force* that pushed back Indian antiquity by almost five thousand years to a distinguished pre-Aryan past, placing ancient Indian civilisation on a line and scale with those of Egypt or Mesopotamia.[67]

Simultaneously Rakhaldas' local fame and credentials came to rest on his writing of the first extended history of Bengal in Bengali (from its prehistoric and ancient period up to the period of British rule).[68] The value of this work has been located in the historical authenticity of its sources and methods—in breaking away from caste and clan genealogies (*kulajis*) towards more 'valid' archaeological evidence, he is seen to have inaugurated a new modernised trend of 'objective' history of Bengal in the mother tongue.[69] The publication of this *History of Bengal* coincided with Rakhaldas' first experimentation with a new genre of fictionalised historical narrative, in a tale he spun around a stone fragment of the Bharhut *stupa*. *Pashaner Katha*, as he called this tale, was the first of the eight historical novels he went on to write in Bengali, opening up a different dimension to his academic professional career.

In retrospect, *Pashaner Katha* has been described as the least 'popular' and the most 'scholarly' of his historical novels.[70] It is the only one where an inert piece of stone takes the place of the standard hero or heroine as the protagonist of the tale, where the narrative is dispersed, slow and self-introspective, lacking an adventurous plot or melodramatic climax. But it is the work which most significantly explores a median ground between 'academic' and 'popular' history, laying itself open to this dual pull. The writer himself cautiously designated it has a 'historical tale': a tale written with 'history' in mind, which was true to its essence but was not itself 'history' in the scientific sense of the term.[71] It was also a work which directly attempted to invoke the image of the Indian nation in its ancient history. It began as an essay which Rakhaldas was asked to write for a new Bengali monthly journal that was floated in 1910 by the historian Hemendraprasad Ghosh. The journal was to be called *Aryavartta* (The Aryan Land), and Rakhaldas' essay was meant to expand on the conception of this name.[72] What was intended as a single essay expanded into a serialised tale in the monthly issues of *Aryavartta* over 1910 to 1911. A mute stone relic was, in the hands of the expert archaeologist, rendered into an oracle of the nation's panoramic past.

The stupa of Bharhut retells its tale

Cunningham had ended his book on the Buddhist remains of Sanchi with the following ode:

Nought but the Topes themselves remain to mock
Time's ceaseless efforts; yet they proudly stand
Silent and lasting up their parent rock,
And still as cities under magic's wand;
Till curious Saxons, from a distant land,
Unlocked the treasures of two thousand years;
And the lone scene is peopled; here a band
Of music wakes the echoes; there the cheers
Of multitudes, alive with human hopes and fears.[73]

Yet the very rigour of his archaeological project would throttle its poetic intentions. In returning history to these antiquities, he placed them within a taxonomy of periods, schools and style that fixed their new 'authentic' meaning. If anything, the distilling of their 'historical' value meant a conscious de-peopling of monuments, their disengagement from their living pasts and human histories. It required a parallel project like that of Rakhaldas, which was willing to step outside the disciplinary boundaries of archaeology while retaining its claims to true knowledge, to indulge in the romantic possibilities raised by Cunningham. *Pashaner Katha* took up the challenge of conjuring up centuries of lost history around the stones of Bharhut, of re-peopling the 'lone' and empty site to make it echo again with 'the cheers of the multitudes'.

Rakhaldas Banerjee's encounter with the Bharhut stones was in their reconstructed form in the Asoka Gallery of the Indian Museum. As an assistant there, he had helped in Bloch's updating of the catalogue of the museum's archaeological collection, providing the details of the materials and measurements of the exhibits.[74] From such a technical cognisance of the monument, he went on to become its historical interlocutor, exploring the romantic potentials of making the stone 'speak'. His story none the less issues out of the site of the museum display: even in its fictionalised form, the written text remains shot through with the effects of this other dominant mode of organising the historical object.

Pashaner Katha also gained an important stamp of scholarly legitimation in the foreword written (for the 1914 edition) by the author's *guru,* Haraprasad Shastri. Not only did the foreword emphasise the years of laborious effort and study through which the author gained access to the histories hidden in stone, it also placed him in the awesome debt of the British scholar-pioneers, most notably James Prinsep and Alexander Cunningham.[75] It was in the acknowledged lineage of the Western enterprise, and his own participation within it, that Rakhaldas Banerjee undertook the writing of this 'historical romance' in Bengali for a home readership.

The pervading theme of the book is the antiquity of stone, its existence in a time span that extended far beyond human history. Thus the story of the stone fragment of Bharhut begins not with the construction of the *stupa*, but at a far anterior time, when it could recall its existence as a speck of sand on the ocean bed, to be returned to land and recast within a mass of red sandstone. It is made to witness the beginnings of human habitation, the conflict between the invading Aryans and the original Dravidian inhabitants of the land, the retreat of the latter to the south of the Vindhyas and, in time, the flooding of the fair-skinned Aryans all over the country, the periodic encircling of jungles and disappearance of humans from the area—before we are brought to the scene of the stone being quarried and carried to a distant spot for the construction of the *stupa*. The crowning moments of the narrative centre around the arrival of the stone slabs on the outskirts of the capital city of the Sunga kingdom of Mahakosala, the proclamations of the Buddhist monks, the encounter with King Dhanabhuti, the supervision of Bactrian-Greek builders and sculptors, the stage-by-stage construction of the *stupa*, and the build-up to its grand public opening.

Let me pause here to consider some of the broader issues embedded within the story. The single dominant theme that keeps recurring is that of the 'golden age' of early Buddhism: a period associated as much with purity of faith and austerity of values, as with the well-being of the people, the magnificence of cities and the artistic grandeur of monuments. The long proclamation by a senior Buddhist *bhikkhu* (monk) at the site gives us a condensed history of Buddhism. We move from its spread under King Asoka and high point in the Maurya era through the decline of the Mauryas, with the Sunga kingdom holding out against resurgent Brahmanism to become an island of peace, refuge and resuscitation for the followers of Buddha.[76] The lavish donation of funds, the completion of the *stupa*, and its consecration with a bodily relic of the Buddha in its inner chamber, recaptures on a smaller arena the full glory of the faith and its civilisation. The narrative also distinctly peaks around this point of history, in the elaboration of the scenes of festivities and religious rejoicing, and in the exuberance of descriptive details.[77]

Thereafter, following the fall of the Sunga kingdom, we are repeatedly confronted with the destruction and desecration of the *stupa* by Brahman antagonists and by waves of foreign invaders—the Sakas, the Huns and the Muslim Turks. Alongside runs the theme of the gradual degeneration of faith and morals within Buddhism (the recourse to idolatry and deviation from all its founding principles) and its progressive disappearance, barring some local pockets. This is punctuated by certain main phases of revival and renewed glory, under the reign of the Kushana ruler Kanishka (first to second century A.D.), and under the Gupta dynasty (fourth to sixth centuries A.D.), which saw the partial restoration, reconsecration and embellishment of the sacred structure. But neither phase could return either the Buddhist religion or the *stupa* to its 'original' grandeur, nor could they reverse the pre-ordained process of the downward slide.

Another significant theme that is periodically interpolated within the narrative, is the controversy concerning the autonomous growth of the arts of sculpture and architecture in ancient India. The choice of a stone from the Bharhut *stupa* involved a necessary engagement with such 'art-historical' issues, within the folds of the story—for by then Bharhut had been instituted not just as an archaeological relic, but as a powerful symbol of India's early artistic excellence. Thus, in Chapters 3 and 4 the story provides us with as detailed a description of the architecture and the sculpted panels as the Cunningham text—as scrutinised by the artists and builders, or as gazed on by the wondering eyes of the public on the first day of the opening of the *stupa*. Even as the theory of the Greek influence on Buddhist art was being overhauled within the new Orientalist and nationalist discourse, the Indo-Greek sculptors (termed the *Yavanas*) make a prominent appearance in Rakhadlas' story, as supervisors and instructors to the local artisans on the construction site. We are told of the unrivalled talent of the *Yavanas* for sculpting human likenesses in stone, as well as the influence of Egyptian or Parthian motifs on the sculptures of the *stupa*.[78] But through dialogues between the supervisors and builders, or through a reconsideration of sculpted items, the author retains the image of the absorption of such new features within a prior, independent Indian art tradition.

This idea would notably assert itself around the issue which Rajendralal Mitra had earlier taken up against Fergusson—the issue of the alleged absence of the art of stone architecture in India prior to the Greek contact. The allegation is contested repeatedly within Rakhaldas' story. We are introduced to the 'surprise' of the splendid stone architecture of the Sunga kingdom through the eyes of the visiting Greek artists, who had been under the mistaken impression that 'Indians' were ignorant of the skills of stone-carving. What is interesting is the way the retrospective, reconstructive vision of the archaeologist is brought into play. Rajendralal Mitra's argument that the 'negation of proof' (the absence of earlier stone remains) could not serve as 'positive proof' is followed up here, through persuasive images of richly carved, elaborate stone structures which were ravaged by invaders and eroded by time, and the survival through chance of wooden architecture from later periods to confuse the future scholar. Thus, for instance, while the masonry of the Maurya and Sunga cities vanished, fragments of wooden buildings constructed later during Kanishka's reign (when the *stupa* was cleared and rebuilt) were discovered in the vicinity during British excavations. This had immediately reinforced the Western theory that the stone *stupa* must have been developed out of such 'pre-existing' wooden models that stood in the area.

Rakhaldas reflects on the tricky nature of archaeological evidence, investing his stone slab with the ultimate authority of a historical 'eyewitness'.

> The past has not left its remains arranged layer by layer for your convenience; in the upheavals of nature, the top layers have gone under, the lower layers have surfaced above, and many layers in between have moved away to other areas. The powers to analyse the movement of history do not belong to all; they can only come from extensive education and years of training and apprenticeship. When the white masters excavated the spot near the southern gateway of the *stupa*, the ornate wooden fragments they found belonged not to a period prior to the stone structure, but to the period of Saka rule. Do not be surprised and disbelieving, when you hear this. I am a witness of past eras, take my word for truth. If I had the ability to measure

time, then, like you, I would have calculated the year, the month, the day....
If I had eyes, then I would have said, I have *seen*, in person....[79]

Again and again, Rakhaldas extols the unique capacity of stone to
speak of distant times, and to know the sole truth about that time. The
stone's authority becomes a surrogate of the author's own. It enabled
him freely to conjure up possibilities in history, around the monument,
without the back-up of concrete archaeological evidence. The stones of
Bharhut, laden with 'archaeological' and 'art-historical' value, could
also be endowed with religious sanctity by invoking the existence of an
original inner chamber (*garbha-griha*) in which was placed a portion of
the bodily relic of Sakyamuni, brought from another *stupa* at Udyan in
the Gandhara region.[80] That inner chamber, in time sealed up and fallen
into disuse, was lost to posterity, as the *stupa* was ransacked and
destroyed by the Saka and Hun invaders. The stone slab regrets that
whatever few traces and signs remained escaped the notice of the
experts during the excavations.

Fig. 2 Bharhut stupa: Ajatacatru pillar (OIOC; British Library)

The *stupa* of Bharhut, as we encounter it in this story, is not fixed within a single 'original' history of its construction. Rather, it is made to stand within a continuous flow of time and events, subjected to several destructions and rebuildings, the initial structure laid open to many deletions and accretions. Indeed, such changes and intrusions in its form became symptomatic of the main historical currents that obsessed the writer—the theme of an embattled, declining Buddhism, or the theme of foreign invasions. We are carried through waves of destruction (the worst of these being the Hun attack), and reconstructions under intermittent Buddhist regimes, with the entire structure being appropriated by Hindu Shaivites in the early medieval period.[81] Then follows a period of anarchy and disintegration, building up to the final plunder of the Muslim invasions.

As in Cunningham's book, here too the history of the Bharhut *stupa* comes to a halt at this point. As the stone loses contact with light and the human world, the nation's history also freezes, till a new group of *Yavanas* (the British) retrieves the ruins and unravels its lost history.[82] From the moment of the Muslim invasions, the narrative jumps rapidly into the moment of the colonial archaeological discovery. For the author, the ruined form of the *stupa* in the Indian Museum stood testimony, not so much to the centuries of mutation as to the final definitive ravage of the Muslim invasion.[83] After years of oblivion, the stones of Bharhut arrive at a new heightened point of self-fulfilment, as they meet the gaze of the British archaeologist and feel the touch of his connoisseurship. Sifting through the different layers of accretions and rebuildings, that expert gaze recognises the antiquity and shape of the 'original' structure. The stones are cleared and handled with the utmost care with which a mother cradles her children.[84] Their story ends with their arrival in the Indian Museum: with this final re-entry into the world of humans, the Bharhut *stupa* is radically reborn as a modern museum relic.

It is in this last metamorphosed, resanctified form that the stone also became a repository of national history. The long and diverse history that it recounted came to stand in for the designated history of *'Bharatbarsha'*, of past peoples who can now be termed *'Bharatbasis'*. The regional, the local and the fragmentary were all recaptured in the singular interests of a composite national history, where the parts (it was claimed) could easily fit into and contain the whole. Both Rakhaldas' narrative and Akshay Maitreya's review of the work the same year, highlight this point:

The stone which occupies the role of the narrator here, is *a stone of India*....
Many may wonder, can a history of a single monument be taken as the
history of the whole of our vast lands. To tackle such objections, the author
has made the stone tell us again and again—that which is the tale of Bharhut
is also the tale of all other places—in every place, every such [ancient]
stone is echoing with the same tale.[85]

That tale was one of the grandeur and decline of the civilisation that
was 'ancient India', of which the age of the Mauryas and early
Buddhism symbolised the climactic peak, and in which the modern
community of the Indian nation located its ancestry. A recent probe into
this process of 'the imaginary institution of India' begged the question
whether 'something that was born in the nineteenth century [the idea of
the Indian nation] could have a biography leading back a
millennium'.[86] Even as it posed the question, it provided an answer—
that the 'reality' of the construct lay, in the end, in the form and force of
the claim. History, to be an effective principle, had to carry the modern
inscription and identity of the nation. The transformation of something
fundamentally tenuous and insecure into something aggressively self-
evident became the mark of success of nationalist ideology. And it was
in this creative period of its formation and self-formulation, that the
fiction of an 'Indian' history most effectively naturalised its presence.

---

[1] An earlier version of this chapter was presented at a seminar on 'Proof and
Persuasion' at the Davis Center for Historical Studies, University of Princeton,
in January 1994. I have greatly benefited from the discussions at that seminar
and from feedbacks at the other seminars where I have presented sections of this
work. A version of this chapter is included in a forthcoming volume of essays
being published by the Davis Center, Princeton.

[2] On ways of studying the historical emergence of disciplines, see Messer-
Davidow, Shumway and Sylvan (eds.), *Knowledges, Historical and Critical
Studies in Disciplinarity* (Charlottesville, 1993). The idea of disciplinarity, as
argued here, directly bears out the Foucauldian notions of power and
knowledge—his projection of 'truth' as 'a system of ordered procedures for the
production, regulation, distribution, circulation and operation of statements'.

[3] For an extended study of his work, see Abu Imam, *Sir Alexander Cunningham and the Beginnings of Indian Archaeology* (Dacca, 1966); and Dilip K. Chakrabarti, *A History of Indian Archaeology* (New Delhi, 1988).

[4] Quoted in Cunningham, *Four reports*, p.ii.

[5] These sets of aquatint engravings, preserved in the Oriental and India Office Collections, London, and the Victoria Memorial, Calcutta, among other places, have been widely reproduced. See, for example, M. Archer, *Early Views of India: the picturesque journeys of Thomas and William Daniell* (London, 1980).

[6] Recounted by Fergusson in the prefaces to his first books, *Picturesque Illustrations of Ancient Architecture in Hindostan* (London, 1848), and *The Rock-Cut Temples of India* (London, 1864).

[7] Pramod Chandra, *On the Study of Indian Art* (Cambridge, Mass., 1983).

[8] Fergusson, *Picturesque Illustrations*, p.iv.

[9] 'On the Study of Indian Architecture', a lecture delivered to a meeting of the Society of Arts, London, 19 December 1866, and published in 1867 by the Science and Art Department, South Kensington Museum, London, for the use of the Schools of Art in the United Kingdom (reprint, Delhi, 1977).

[10] Ibid., p.11.

[11] Ibid., p.10.

[12] Four independent groups were formed in Bombay, Madras, Calcutta and North-Western Provinces to undertake this detailed work of documentation; and superintendents of the newly-established schools of art were instructed to involve local students in the preparation of drawings and casts of ancient Indian art forms. Alongside museums in England, museums and art schools in India were meant to receive a 'just share' of such photographs, drawings and casts. In this, the idea was not only to acquaint Indians with their own antiquities and artistic heritage but also 'to place before the Native artisan [the prime concern of British art educationists] the best examples of his country's skill...to conserve for his use the monuments of an artistic power which still lives in him....'

[13] Archaeological Survey of India, *Report on the illustration of the Archaic Architecture of India* by J. Forbes Watson (London, 1869)—containing memorandum by Mr. Fergusson regarding the architectural objects in India, of which it is desirable photographs and casts should be obtained; letter by Mr. Fergusson, referring to the scheme for the conservation and representation of ancient monuments in India.

[14] Such a three-part classification is made by Alois Riegl, 'The modern cult of monuments: its character and its origin', in *Oppositions*, 25, 1982.

[15] *Report on the illustration of the Archaic Architecture of India*, memorandum by General Cunningham on the archaeological remains of India.

[16] See his Introduction written in 1871 to his Four reports, pp.i-xliii.

[17] Ibid., pp.xviii-xix. This is quoted and restated in a recent study of early British Orientalists: O.P. Kejariwal, *The Asiatic Society of Bengal and the Discovery of India's Past* (Delhi, 1988).

[18] Introduction to Four reports, pp.vii-xix.

[19] The metaphor of 'mapping' and the analogy with the Trigonometrical Survey, invoked in Cunningham's own memorandum of 1861, appears again in Dilip Chakrabarti's evaluation of his surveys. He writes, 'One cannot help feeling that his work did for Indian archaeology what the Trigonometrical Survey achieved for the Indian land mass. Things were mapped out on a grand scale in both cases', Chakrabarti, *A History of Indian Archaeology*, p.116.

[20] Fa Hien had travelled from the banks of the upper Indus to the mouth of the Ganges between 399 and 413 A.D.; and Hiuen Tsang had spent nearly fifteen years, from 629 to 645 A.D., studying the famous books and visiting the holy places of Buddhism in India. The accounts of these Chinese pilgrims became

known to European scholarship only in this period through French translations. Stanislas Julien's translation of Hiuen Tsang's travels was published in two volumes in Paris in 1857-8.

[21] Alexander Cunningham, *The Ancient Geography of India*, I, *The Buddhist Period, including the campaigns of Alexander and the travels of Hwen Thsang* (London, 1871), Preface, pp.iii-xx.

[22] On the Gandhara sculptures, the European fascination with them and the controversy they excited concerning the so-called Greek influence on Indian art history, see, for instance, Partha Mitter, *Much Maligned Monsters: history of European reaction to Indian art* (Oxford, 1977).

[23] Alexander Cunningham, 'An account of the discovery of the ruins of the Buddhist city of Samkassa', *Journal of the Royal Asiatic Society*, 7, 1843. Cited in Chakrabarti, *A History of Indian Archaeology*, pp.43-4, 51.

[24] Fergusson, *On the Study of Indian Architecture*, pp.8-9.

[25] For an extended discussion of this theory, see Mitter, *Much Maligned Monsters*, pp.256-67.

[26] Alexander Cunningham, 'Proposed archaeological investigation', *Journal of the Asiatic Society of Bengal*, 17 (1848), pp.535-6.

[27] Cunningham, 'An account of...the ruins of the Buddhist city of Samkassa'.

[28] Alexander Cunningham, *The Bhilsa Topes* (London, 1854).

[29] The most extensive of these would be the work of General F.C. Maisey, resulting in his book, *Sanchi and Its Remains, a Full Description of the Ancient Buildings, Sculptures and Inscriptions* (London, 1892). This was followed by the massive three-volume work of J.H. Marshall and Alfred Foucher, *The Monuments of Sanchi* (Calcutta, 1913-14).

[30] The history of the 'discovery' of the Amaravati marbles, their transference first to the Madras Museum, and then to the India Museum, London, where they lay abandoned before they were 'rediscovered' by Fergusson, is discussed in Bernard Cohn's article, 'The transformation of objects into artifacts, antiquities and art in nineteenth-century India', in Barbara Stoler Miller (ed.), *The Powers of Art* (Delhi, 1991).

[31] This was the main project of a book he entitled, *Tree and Serpent Worship or Illustrations of Mythology and Art in India in the First and Fourth Centuries after Christ from the Sculptures of the Buddhist topes at Sanchi and Amaravati* (London, 1868).

[32] Alexander Cunningham, *The Stupa of Bharhut, a Buddhist Monument Ornamented with Numerous Sculptures Illustrative of Buddhist Legend and History* (London, 1879).

[33] Benedict Anderson on the restoration of the ancient cites of Borobodur, Angkor or Pagan, in *Imagined Communities* (London, New York, 1991), p.179.

[34] James Fergusson, *History of Indian and Eastern architecture* (new edition, London, 1899), pp.86-7.

[35] See, for example, E.B. Havell, *Indian Sculpture and Painting* (London, 1908), which pointedly sought to replace the earlier 'archaeological' approach with a new 'aesthetic' appraisal of the subject.

[36] It has been suggested that despite it greater concern with aesthetics, the modern discipline of art history (no less than that of archaeology), constructs its objects of study as 'evidential in nature', guided typically by the hypothesis that 'in a number of determinate and reconstructible ways, an artwork is reflective...of the original historical circumstances of its production', Donald Preziozi, 'Seeing through art history', in Messer-Davidow, Shumway and Sylvan (eds.), *Knowledges, Historical and Critical Studies in Disciplinarity*, p.215.

[37] Cunningham, *The Stupa of Bharhut*, pp.3-4.

[38] Ibid., pp.14-17, 127.

[39] Ibid., pp.4-14.

[40] Among the main sources he used were Spence Hardy's *Manual of Buddhism*; Rhys David's *Buddhist Birth Stories*; and translations of *Jataka* tales of the twelfth-century text, *Katha Sarit Sagara*, or H.H. Wilson's translation of the *Vishnu Purana*.

[41] The later arrival of images of Buddha in Buddhist art of the Mahayana is noted as a sign of 'corruption' and descent into idolatry.

[42] Cunningham, *The Stupa of Bharhut*, pp.v-vii, 4-5.

[43] As Benedict Anderson analyses in *Imagined Communities*, pp.178-85, such thoroughness of description and documentation was an essential part of a colonial state's programme of creating, under its control, a human and material landscape of 'perfect visibility' and 'total surveyabilty'.

[44] Against the allegation that the scheme carried with it 'a certain aroma of vandalism [fancy carting away Stonehenge!]', Cunningham wrote, 'I am willing to accept the aroma since I have *saved* all the more important sculptures. Of those that were left behind, every stone that was removable has since been "carted away" by the people for building purposes', *The Stupa of Bharhut*, p.vii.

[45] *Preservation of National Monuments*, Reports of H.H. Cole,Curator of Ancient Monuments in India, 1881-4, First Report, p.11.

[46] This transformation is plotted out in the centenary history of the institution, *The Indian Museum, 1814-1914* (Calcutta, 1914).

[47] In fact, a copy of the book was kept in the gallery for reference; and the *Catalogue and Handbook of the Archaeological Collections of the Indian Museum* (Calcutta, 1883) by Superintendent John Anderson, based its entire lengthy description of the display on Cunningham's account.

[48] Referred to in Sourindranath Roy, 'Indian archaeology from Jones to Marshall', *Ancient India* 9 (1953), pp.4-28.

[49] The aim of a work like *The Antiquities of Orissa*, vols. I and II (Calcutta, 1875 and 1880), was closely framed by Lord Canning's directives—to describe and investigate the history and tradition associated with the ancient monuments of India, and to emphasise any light which these monuments may throw on the social, religious and cultural history of the period to which they belonged.

[50] Rajendralal, *The Antiquities of Orissa*, vol.II, pp.5-6.

[51] Rajendralal, *The Antiquities of Orissa*, vol.I, pp.60, 77-8.

[52] Ibid., pp.15-16, 22-3.

[53] The choice of Orissa itself underlined this point—for, in Rajendralal's view, it was Orissa's insulation in time, space and history (particularly her insulation from the Muslim past) which made her architecture the 'purest' and most 'pristine' relics of the national art tradition.

[54] In 1884 it occasioned an entire book by Fergusson, *Archaeology in India, with Especial Reference to the Works of Babu Rajendralal Mitra* (reprint New Delhi, 1970).

[55] Ibid., pp.vi-vii, 3-4.

[56] Ibid., pp.4-7.

[57] Chakrabarti, *A History of Indian Archaeology*, p.100. Thus the exclusive area of expertise set up by Fergusson as the 'discipline' of archaeology is carried over into the history that is accorded to the discipline.

[58] Fergusson, *Archaeology in India*, p.5.

[59] This reversal of trends and approaches has been dealt with in detail in my book, *The Making of a New 'Indian' Art: artists, aesthetics and nationalism in Bengal* (Cambridge, 1992), pp.146-84.

[60] Lord Curzon, Ancient Monuments in India, *Annual Progress Report of the Archaeological Survey Circle*, 31 March 1900.

[61] Guha-Thakurta, *The Making of a New 'Indian' Art*, pp.185-301.

[62] This thesis is argued out in a set of essays now compiled in a book, *Sagarika* (Calcutta, 1986).

[63] *Sirajuddaulah* (1896), and *Mir Kasim* (1906).

[64] *Aitihasik Chitra*, which he began in 1899-1900, which was continued under a new editor from 1907-10.

[65] See, for example, his article, 'Pratnavidya', *Sahitya*, 23rd year, 1319 (1912).

[66] Many of these histories, like a large portion of Rakhaldas' scholarly output, were published posthumously after his premature death in 1930.

[67] The complete findings and conclusions of the author have only recently been made available with the publication of his manuscript; *Mohenjodaro: a forgotten report* (Varanasi, 1984).

[68] Rakhaldas Banerjee, *Bangalar Itihas*, vols. 1 and 2 (Calcutta, 1321-24/1914-17).

[69] Dilip Kumar Biswas, 'Prachin Bharat-Itihascharchay Rakhaldas Bandopadhyay', in K.K. Dasgupta (ed.), *Shatavarsher Aaloye Rakhaldas Bandopadhyay* (Calcutta, 1990), pp.22-3.

[70] Pratap Chandra Chanda, 'Aitihasik Upanyas Rachanay Rakhaldas', in ibid., p.47.

[71] Rakhaldas Bandopadhyay, preface to the first edition of *Pashaner Katha* (Calcutta, 1914; reprint 1990). The English title of the book used the label, 'a historical romance'.

[72] Preface to the first edition.

[73] Cunningham, *The Bhilsa Topes*, quoted by Chakrabarti, *A History of Indian Archaeology*, p.56.

[74] *Supplementary Catalogue of the Archaeological Collection of the Indian Museum, Calcutta* by the late Theodore Bloch (Calcutta, 1911).

[75] Banerjee, *Pashaner Katha*, p.iii.

[76] Ibid., pp.13-16.

[77] Ibid., pp.23-48.

[78] Ibid., pp.20-1.

[79] Ibid., pp.60-1.

[80] Ibid., pp.44-5.

[81] Ibid., pp.117-9.

[82] This sense of the Muslim invasions being the drastic cut-off point in Indian history is more sharply expressed in the author's next historical novel, *Sasanka* (Calcutta, 1321/1914), which is set in the Gupta period. He wrote in its preface, 'We [Indians] were alive before the Muslim invasions; in being conquered by the Muslims we have died....' And one of his main reasons for writing such historical tales, he said, was to recapture for his people a spirited time from India's 'living' past.

[83] *Pashaner Katha*, p.120.

[84] Ibid., pp.123-4.

[85] Akshay Kumar Maitreya, 'Pashaner Katha', *Manasi* (Aashar 1321/1914). This review was included at the end of the second edition of the book when it was republished in 1923, and was seen to serve as its best preamble; *Pashaner Katha*, pp.128, 134.

[86] Sudipta Kaviraj, 'The imaginary institution of India', Partha Chatterjee and Gyan Pandey (eds.), *Subaltern Studies*, VII (Delhi, 1992), pp.16-18.

Chapter Three

PAINTING AND UNDERSTANDING MUGHAL ARCHITECTURE

G.H.R. Tillotson

In the preface to his travel memoirs, published in 1793, William Hodges observed that English readers had been furnished with much scholarly writing on the laws, religion and polity of India, 'but of the face of the country, of its arts, and natural productions', he lamented, 'little has yet been said'. To supply this deficiency in what he goes on to call, more succinctly, 'the topographical department', was the object of his book and—we may infer—of his three-year tour in India which it describes.[1]

To the modern ear, the idea that natural and artificial productions belong together in a single 'department' might sound odd, and it is a reminder of the English aesthetic values of Hodges's time: though we may now think of him as having played an important role in the early investigation of India's architecture, for Hodges himself it was understood that buildings were not to be separated from their natural contexts, that any building was to be viewed as one element in a wider physical environment. This approach to architecture was fashionable at the time; it was eloquently summarised in the same year by the aesthetic theorist Richard Payne Knight when he insisted that a building is 'a mere component part of what you see'.[2] Hodges's adherence to this approach explains why, in his pictures, although a building may provide the primary subject-matter, he invariably includes some indication of its immediate natural surroundings, even to the point of obscuring our view. We might wonder whether, in consequence, his pictures tell us much about Indian buildings in a 'faithful and authentic' manner, as he insisted,[3] or whether they merely record a moment in English taste (or whether they can do both at once). Or we might imagine an Indian voice—perhaps that of the architect of one of his subjects—objecting 'If you show it in that way you miss the point; you have stressed all the wrong things; that is not what I meant at all!' And then we might consider what authority we should attach to such a voice.

This chapter, then, is about how architecture is understood; specifically it compares an English and an Indian approach. I am not building monoliths: both English and Indian approaches have no doubt always been complex, varied and changing. But each of the two particular approaches which I consider here is durable, in the sense that, though historically situated, it includes ideas which are not restricted to the period of its own formulation. The two approaches are very different from each other, and yet for a period between the late eighteenth and early nineteenth centuries they were applied to the same objects, namely buildings in India, including those produced in the Mughal Empire.

I argue that these two approaches are reflected in the manner in which buildings were represented in English and Indian pictures of them. I am not supposing any straightforward reflective relationship between representation and perception, since both English and Indian paintings are artistic products themselves which are subject to their own conventions and traditions besides those connected with understanding architecture (and these pictorial matters form a part of the account). But I do suggest that in these complex images we can nevertheless discern underlying understandings of architecture itself.[4]

In English painting, in the late eighteenth century, architecture assumed a much greater importance as a subject for its own sake, rather than as a setting for the depiction of, say, a person or an action; but even then, buildings frequently remained parts of landscapes. The change of emphasis marked a decisive step in the development of a distinct English landscape school, itself one aspect of the rise of that pervasive and durable English aesthetic which we call the Picturesque. The representation of Indian buildings at this time follows that formula, in spite of the foreign nature of the subject-matter. Enough has been written about picturesque images of India[5] to make only a brief discussion of this part of the argument necessary here. The earliest and most prolific English landscape painters in India were William Hodges and Thomas and William Daniell, and a single pair of examples can be used to illustrate ubiquitous features of their work.

In William Hodges's aquatint of the tomb of Makhdum Shah Daulat at Maner in Bihar (Fig. 1),[6] the main building is seen from a distance and occupies only a small portion of the picture surface. It is thoroughly integrated into a natural setting: across the picture plane there is an alternation of natural and artificial elements (tree-building-

Fig. 1 William Hodges, *A View of the Mosque at Mounheer*, aquatint, 1787 (IOLR)

Fig. 2 Thomas and William Daniell, *The Mausoleum of Mucdoom Shah Dowlut, at Moneah*, aquatint, 1796 (IOLR)

tree-building-tree), and with it an alternation of colour between green and brown. Nature and architecture are not just mixed but answer each other in a single composition: the clouds mass behind the buildings to emphasise and echo their silhouette, while the foreground tree parts to frame the entrance to the gate.

In the slightly later aquatint of the same subject by Thomas and William Daniell (Fig. 2),[7] the tomb is given greater prominence and the vegetation is reduced, but the building is still integrated into a composition with its surroundings: it hangs on the horizon like a bead on a string, and is held in the middle ground by the dark shadow in the foreground and the dark cloud behind.

Like Hodges, the Daniells have observed the tomb from an oblique angle, and this choice is also for compositional purposes. The picturesque aesthetic favours irregular and varied objects, and thus a symmetrical building—like Makhdum Shah Daulat's tomb—is not an ideal subject. As the picturesque theorist William Gilpin observed in 1792:

> A piece of Palladian architecture may be elegant in the last degree. The proportion of its parts—the propriety of its ornaments—and the symmetry of the whole, may be highly pleasing. But if we introduce it in a picture, it immediately becomes a formal object and ceases to please. Should we wish to give it picturesque beauty, we must use the mallet instead of the chisel: we must beat down one half of it, deface the other, and throw the mutilated members around in heaps. In short, from a smooth building we must turn it into a rough ruin. No painter, who had the choice of the two objects, would hesitate a moment.[8]

Accordingly, both Hodges and the Daniells frequently did choose ruined buildings as fit subjects. But sometimes, as in this case, they were attracted to buildings which were relatively intact and even symmetrical. The problem with a symmetrical building from the picturesque perspective is that it is compositionally complete in itself, because its parts echo each other. But, if it is represented obliquely, it can be made to create a two-dimensional form which is not symmetrical, which is irregular, and which therefore requires the presence of other objects to complete the compositional balance of the picture. By showing the tomb from an angle, the Daniells have made it look not inwards on its own centre, but outwards to the right; and this rightwards movement then has to be checked by the introduction of those masses of shadow and cloud to the left, thus ensuring that the building becomes not a self-contained object but 'a mere component part of what you see'.

Such disruption of architectural symmetry not only assists the integration of buildings into landscape, it also lends them scenic qualities of their own. This transfer of qualities is again typical of picturesque ideas. For William Gilpin, landscape was artificial, whether literally so—as in a landscape garden or painting—or metaphorically—since natural landscapes could be described and appreciated as though they were designed by the artist Nature. And if landscape is artificial, so architecture can have scenic qualities—an idea in English architectural thought which goes back to Robert Adam, for whom:

> The rise and fall, the advance and recess with other diversity of form...have the same effect in architecture that hill and dale, foreground and distance, swelling and sinking have in landscape.[9]

The oblique angle and consequent asymmetry of shape in the pictures, make the buildings seem more natural, more proximate in form to the trees and hills which often surround them.

The approach to architecture which underlies such images is evidently one in which buildings are seen as continuous with nature, not as objects of a unique class. It is also an approach which emphasises their sculptural qualities: they are shapely objects. Thirdly, it assumes they are things to be seen, and depicted, from particular points of view—and given their shapeliness it is usually from the exterior. Natural, shapely and pictorial—buildings can often be seen to have such qualities, but especially in the eyes of those whose concerns about architecture itself are overwhelmingly aesthetic.

A different set of priorities emerge from Indian paintings of buildings. There is a similarity with the English case in that it was especially in the period under review that architecture emerged as a major primary subject in painting. Of course, architectural elements had long been ubiquitous in Indian painting, but usually to provide a setting for the primary subject (which might be an action described in a text, or a courtly topos); and though such images might accurately reproduce architectural details or decoration, they rarely show actual and identifiable buildings. Even in the exceptional cases (as, for instance, in some Mughal and some Mewar paintings) where we are able to identify, for example, a particular courtyard in a palace, the architecture is still included as a backdrop to another, perhaps courtly, subject: such paintings are not in the first instance records of buildings. From the period under review, however, there survives a small but significant genre of Indian painting devoted to the representation of buildings themselves. Again, a discussion of a few examples will reveal some common characteristics.

Taking first a late eighteenth-century Rajasthani representation of Akbar's tomb at Sikandra (Fig. 3),[10] a Western observer in particular will immediately be struck by the multiple points of view; some parts of the complex are shown in elevation, others in plan and others again in perspective, and yet all of these elements are united into a coherent design.

Further consideration of these mixed angles of view reveals that the choice of them is far from random: each element of the architectural ensemble is depicted from an angle which emphasises its purpose, the role that it plays in the architectural complex. The main (southern) gateway, for example, serves in the actual complex as a point of entry and as a screen in front of the tomb proper; and in the painting it is depicted at the bottom of the page, where the eye enters the plane, and in elevation, like a screen. This is indeed the gate's characteristic appearance, or, to put it another way, how we experience it in reality: as we use the gate we are likely to be struck most by the appearance of its outer face, and by its giving us access to the rest of the complex. Similarly, the southern front of the tomb itself—which in reality acts as a further point of entry and screen—and the northern pavilion—which serves to close a vista from the tomb—are here both also shown in elevation. The main structure of the tomb is the actual complex's central part, and a part which we walk around; and our experience of its three-dimensionality is stressed in the painting where—more fully than any other part—it is shown in perspective. The garden or *charbagh* is shown in plan, reminding us that it is a flat and regularly formed space, and rendering unmistakable the simple fact that it is a *charbagh*—a type which is defined by its plan.

Stuart Cary Welch saw in the whole design a resemblance to a mandala,[11] but while the formal similarity is compelling, it might be coincidental. Rather than overlaying an extra meaning on his subject, the artist may have been attempting to stress its own. The pattern arises from the emphasis on the plan, and the artist focused on this because it is precisely the plan of a *charbagh* which gives it its meaning, which makes it operate as an image of paradise, an image central to the working of a tomb. The painting, in short, is a visual representation of the building's function and meaning. It shows the whole of the complex because all of its parts contribute to its meaning.

Fig. 3 Jaipur Artist, *Akbar's Tomb at Sikandra*, watercolour, c.1780 (private collection)

In this context it is significant that the natural environment is all but excluded. The gardens are prominent, but they may be considered part of the architectural scheme; otherwise the natural context is reduced to thin strips of sky and land along the top and bottom of the page. It is as though the artist has understood and wanted to show the quality of a *charbagh*: its walls enclose it and isolate its fertile interior from the environmentally hostile world, and the artist has made this architectural boundary into his picture's border.

We encounter here a very different way of showing from that embodied in an English picture of a comparable subject,[12] which might be said to record a single view or act of seeing. The Indian picture corresponds to our visual experience only if we include the dimension of time: we cannot in life see all the parts at once, but we can explore them in turn; and the painting draws together our sequence of perceptions and understandings of the various elements (in this sense it is a narrative painting). Where an English artist would situate us with respect to the building as one-time viewers, the Indian artist reveals the building to us as patient interpreters.

This painting is not unique in Indian art of the period. Representations of temples frequently concentrate on the plan, on the images of the gods, and on the tanks: on those parts, that is, which are most important to the building's meaning; and the artist will adopt

Fig. 4 Bengali (?) Artist, *Temple at Madhusudan and Rath, Bausi*, watercolour, 1818 (RAS)

multiple perspectives in order to accommodate them all.[13] In an early nineteenth-century view of a temple in Bihar (Fig. 4),[14] we see the gateway from the outside as if about to use it, and the ranges around the courtyard as if from its centre. The picture is a narrative record of a series of visual experiences over time. Furthermore the temple is shown as if (like an actual temple) it is considered complete in itself: there is no attempt to show its urban setting. The *rath* is shown on a scale which has regard to its religious importance not to visual realism.[15]

In images such as these, buildings are seen not as quasi-natural, or continuous with their environment, but as avowedly artificial, as isolated places apart. They are not shapely, formal objects, but spatial, ordered areas. They are not pictorial, things to be looked at, but comprehensible, things to be understood. In short, such images suggest an approach to architecture which is less aesthetic than functionalist.

It is proposed, then, that the few pictures so far discussed reflect not only two distinct pictorial traditions but also two profoundly different approaches to architecture, which might crudely be labelled as, respectively, formalist and functionalist. In further support of this hypothesis is the minor detail that the English artists mentioned, whilst being attentive to the forms of the buildings they drew, were frequently confused or ignorant about their functions. Hodges, for example, described the tomb at Maner as a mosque, and when he drew the Jami Masjid at Jaunpur he called it a tomb.[16] To be generous, one should point out that the Maner tomb has an associated mosque, and the Jaunpur mosque has an associated tomb; but anyone interested in function would soon master that small complication. By contrast, an Indian order of priorities is perhaps reflected in the circumstance that the Maner tomb is known as the Choti Dargah (or little tomb) in distinction to the adjacent great or Bari Dargah—the architecturally far less impressive but spiritually more important tomb of Yahia Shah Maneri.

But these points are anecdotal. For a more serious trial of the hypothesis, I turn now to some further pictures. But rather than adducing more comparisons between English and Indian views, I am concerned with a group of works which present a test case, because they were made by Indian artists for English patrons. There exists a specialist genre of 'Company' paintings devoted to the representation of Indian, and especially Mughal, buildings. Some examples of this genre survive from before the end of the eighteenth century,[17] but as

Mildred Archer has pointed out, the vogue for pictures of the Taj Mahal and other great Mughal monuments expanded greatly following the capture of Delhi and Agra from the Marathas by the British in 1803, and the consequent greater accessibility of the buildings for European tourists.[18]   Not all visitors had the time or the accomplishments required to make their own images, and so they turned to local Indian artists to supply them with records. The genre flourished from 1803 for about four decades, and a substantial body of work survives.[19] My case is that in these pictures, the Indian artists have moved towards their new patrons by adopting elements of the English style; but that some pictorial conventions are more readily assimilable than the understanding of architecture which underlies them, and that in important respects these works sustain Indian modes of seeing and showing. In particular, very few come at all close to being accurately describable as picturesque.

Many of the distinctive features of these pictures are already apparent in early examples (such as Fig.5).[20] Most strikingly, the artist has relinquished the aim to show all the significant parts of the architectural complex simultaneously, and has abandoned the multi-perspective style which facilitated that aim. We have here a record of only as much of the Taj Mahal as one can see at once, and the use of single-point perspective. And so the artist has apparently abandoned what, by the hypothesis, was the central aim, to explain the building.

However, while the Taj Mahal has certainly here become a thing to be seen, more than understood, it has not become a fully sculptural object. The faintness of the modelling means that it is not given full solidity, and the picture retains a two-dimensional quality. More arrestingly, there has been no attempt to depict its physical context or natural environment. The building's artificiality, its separateness, is if anything all the more emphatic for the degree of realism: the building is positively torn from its context and set to float on a blank sheet. From such an image, we could not possibly deduce even the building's size.

The care in the perspective drawing—especially in the rendering of the pavement—is almost fanatical. It is a faultless exercise. And yet there are aspects of the treatment which undermine the idea that this is what one might see from a chosen point of view. The artist has been concerned to include every detail of the building's surface: every element of its decoration is included and given equal weight. If in fact we stand on such a spot, we cannot see every detail, and certainly not all parts equally: to see the details we have to approach the building. And so while evidently the artist was very much (indeed obsessively)

Fig. 5 Delhi or Agra Artist, *West Side of the Taaj Mahl at Agra*, watercolour, c.1808 (IOLR)

concerned with the visible, he was not concerned with replicating a single act of seeing. The picture does not, like an English view,[21] record one given sight, but combines elements that we can see from afar with those we see from nearby. This synoptic record is reminiscent of a long tradition in Indian art: of the multiple action found not only in Mughal and other Indian court painting, but stretching back to the earliest examples of Indian narrative art. The English values are not so much adopted as modified to make them approximate established Indian ones.

This particular image is typical of a large number of similar angled views of the Taj Mahal.[22] The similarities suggest an important detail of working practice. Close inspection reveals that none of the images is a precise copy of another, but clearly some are closely modelled on others. They are not therefore images drawn from life or even necessarily based on sketches made in situ, as English pictures were. The use of earlier examples as models led to the establishment of certain stock images.

Frequently pictures (including this one) were contained in albums. Typically an album would contain a number of views of the Taj Mahal, including some details of the decorative work, and then an assortment

Fig. 6 Delhi or Agra Artist, *Entrance Gate to the Emperor Ackbar's Tomb at Secundra*, watercolour, c.1808 (IOLR)

Fig. 7 Latif of Agra, *Tomb of Ittameh ud Dowlah near Agra*, watercolour, c.1820 (IOLR)

of views of other Mughal monuments (and sometimes less closely related buildings). The Taj Mahal was by far the favourite subject.

Another which was usually included (and which can be illustrated from the same album) is Akbar's tomb at Sikandra, and its southern gate (Fig.6).[23] Contrasting this image with the earlier Indian view of the subject (Fig.3) shows clearly what has changed and what has not. The gate is not here shown as part of a natural scene in the English manner; it is still a clearly artificial, isolated object, taken from its physical context and filling the page, in the Indian manner. On the other hand, it is no longer shown as contributing to a whole meaningful architectural ensemble; it has become an object to be seen, to lie under the eye—in this regard rejecting the Indian for an English approach. But not fully, since it is still not seen as a shapely object, in spite of the single-point perspective: it is turned into a two-dimensional coloured pattern, and seen simultaneously from near and afar. Crucially, there is no attempt here at an illusion of reality. This is unmistakably a made picture; no observer could mistake it for an Albertian window onto the world. Much more frankly than any English image of the period, it records an idea of the building; it makes no pretence to being a complete account of our experience. In thus suggesting that the building is not reducible to the visual, it retains something of an Indian approach to architecture, in spite of the adoption of certain Western pictorial conventions.

Another favoured subject of the school was the tomb of Itimad-ud-Daulah in Agra (Fig.7).[24] This picture bears all the usual hallmarks of the style, and without enumerating them again it may be worth observing that the extraordinarily rich surface decoration on this building lends itself to the Company artist's meticulous manner, and that in recording every slight detail of it with equal care, the artist has again underplayed the overall sculptural form of the building and created instead a brilliant flat pattern—a pattern which does not correspond to any single visual experience of the actual building, but which combines distant and close views. The effect is even more emphatic in views of the building's interior (Fig.8),[25] where the play between perspective drawing and flat patterning verges on the hypnotic. Both these pictures are attributed to Latif of Agra, one of the very few artists of the school whose names are recorded. His work is always of remarkable quality and became something of a model for later practitioners.

Though views of the Agra buildings predominate in these collections (and the Moti Masjid in the Agra Fort is another common subject) buildings in other Mughal cities are also treated in the same way. Favourite subjects included certain parts of the imperial complex at Fatehpur Sikri (especially Sheikh Salim Chishti's tomb) and, in Delhi, the Jami Masjid of Shah Jahan (Fig.9).[26] Isolated on its plateau, the Jami Masjid, more than many other buildings, lends itself to the Indian artist's approach, and certainly it presented a challenge to the English picturesque artist. The Daniells were capable of many drastic rearrangements to convey a sense of natural context, but not even they would introduce trees or grassy slopes into the mosque's courtyard. In their own aquatint view of the building, they could scarcely avoid its symmetry and isolation (Fig.10).[27] Yet the comparison is again instructive. The Daniells have shown the building not from straight in front to emphasise its symmetry (as the Indian artist has) but slightly obliquely, subtly disrupting the rhythm of its openings. The courtyard is animated by a strong contrast of light and shade, and the large expanse of sky is filled with an irregular pattern of cloud. By sitting on its plateau, the Jami Masjid may (inconveniently for the Daniells) escape proximity to such obvious natural features as trees, but it cannot escape the most pervasive natural element—light—and the Daniells have made the most of this. The Indian artists made the least of it: their backgrounds are not skies, and there are few shadows. Their pictures are evenly lit, for they are lit not by the sun but by the mind.

Fig. 8 Latif of Agra, *Interior of the Tomb of Ittamed ud Dowlah*, watercolour, c.1820 (IOLR)

Fig. 9 Latif of Agra, *Juma Masjid or Grand Mosque of Delhi*, watercolour, c.1820 (IOLR)

Fig. 10 Thomas and William Daniell, *The Jummah Masjed, Delhi*, aquatint, 1797 (IOLR)

As already noted, an evident and standard feature of these Company paintings is the complete mastery of single-point perspective, and since such a method had not hitherto been a major preoccupation among Indian artists this is worthy of comment, though it is problematical. It is generally supposed that the artists learnt perspective drawings from British engineers.[28] It has to be acknowledged that British engineers did not produce drawings of buildings sufficiently like to serve as models for the Indian artists: even when engaged in surveying buildings, they were usually more interested in producing measured plans than in perspective views. However, it is possible that Indian artists received from the engineers instruction in the techniques of Western draughtmanship. Certainly, images of buildings made by the Indian assistants of surveyors do have important stylistic affinities with the pictures under review, including the preference for frontal perspective, even detailing, and lack of context.[29]

Paintings like those discussed, though numerous, are not the only kind of image of buildings from the period. A remarkable project from the end of the period is the illustrated text of Ram Raz's commentary on the *Manasara*, entitled *An Essay on the Architecture of the Hindoos*, published in 1834. An attempt by an Indian author to explain the principles of Indian architecture from the basis of its own textual tradition, for the benefit of an English audience (indeed sponsored by the Royal Asiatic Society), this exercise stands between two cultures in a manner comparable to Company painting. The text is peppered with comparisons between Indian and Western classical architecture at the level of detail and that of logical structure, as though Ram Raz meant his text to be analogous to a European rationalist treatise on the classical tradition.

The accompanying plates also appear to follow that model: the pattern books of the classical orders. They show not views of actual buildings but specimen parts, offered not as fragments existing in the world but as archetypes—the building blocks for possible constructions, be they a column, a base, an entablature, or more complex elements such as a portico or a *gopura* of twelve storeys (Fig.11).[30] We see here a much more thorough adoption of a Western method of analysis and representation. But, compared with the picturesque, it is a Western method which is perhaps more readily assimilable to an Indian observer, since it focuses on architecture's own internal structures of meaning rather than on the action of seeing

Fig. 11 Indian Artist (for Ram Raz), *A Portico of Four Columns*, pen and ink with wash, 1824, (RAS)

Fig. 12 Delhi or Agra Artist, *Tomb of Hoomauyoon Bad Shah*, watercolour, c.1820 (IOLR)

buildings, and it involves a style of representation which detaches architecture from any physical context. So, the Western approach which is here more thoroughly adopted is one which approximates closely to what I have defined as an Indian approach of the period; at least it is an approach which presents fewer conceptual differences than does the picturesque.

Were Indian artists, then, incapable of reproducing the picturesque style? Not quite. There are some pictures, albeit few, in which the characteristic features of the approach have been adopted: a magnificent view of Humayun's Tomb of c.1820 is one example (Fig.12).[31] In some cases the wholesale adoption of the picturesque was the result of a simple process of copying from an English print.[32] But this is not true of every case. The picturesque aesthetic was not untransferable. That it was transferred so rarely suggests that it made no great appeal to the sensibility of the Indian artists. It would also be wrong to assume that there was a development over time towards an adoption of the picturesque: some of the more successful and original Indian exercises in the style date from the middle of the period; while towards its end, artists produced in very large quantities images of buildings which—while they represent a decline in technical accomplishment—replicate the idiom established much earlier by Latif and his contemporaries. The Indian vision was as persistent as the English vision.

My argument is that images like those discussed do not only represent varying pictorial traditions; they indicate profoundly different understandings of architecture in general and of Mughal buildings in particular. From a body of pictorial work emerge two accounts of Mughal architecture. I stress again that I do not suppose them to be the only possible accounts: it would be a simple matter to find others, including other English and Indian accounts; they are *one* English and *one* Indian account. But, the comparison between them raises the question whether students of Mughal architecture itself, who seek to understand it, have reason to prefer one of these accounts as being more accurately descriptive. Does either have a greater authority?

To some post-structuralist critics such questions might seem naive (and to a pragmatist meaningless), implying as they do the possibility of reaching a central account based on an impartial perception of the material. For some, given the impossibility of establishing such an account, and the existence only of a set of competing readings from competing perspectives, the question of choosing between them rests solely with the present purposes of the reader. But even while accepting that we can never in practice arrive at such a central account, I suggest that we can identify given accounts as being closer to, or further from, being one—as approaching or disregarding what Umberto Eco has called 'the intention of the work'.[33] Avoiding the fallacy of authorial intent, but equally avoiding the chaos that ensues from claiming pre-eminence for the reader (and thus for multiple readers), this idea of Eco's restores the importance of historical and cultural context. It gives us reason to prefer, to choose between given accounts, and to use them to make new and better ones.

Which of these two accounts of Mughal architecture, then, should we prefer? The metaphor of proximity sets up a claim for the Indian ones, and this is further supported by one of the distinctions made here: namely, the suggestion that the Indian artists are more concerned to reveal the building to us (even if, in the case of the Company artists, revealing chiefly its visible aspects) while the English artists record an act of seeing. This could be paraphrased by saying that the English artists address the viewer while the Indian artists address the object.

There are two grounds for hesitation. First, it is by no means self-evident that the best account of any system is one from within, beset as it may be by deceit or self-deception. But whilst cautious on that ground, we can at least rely on an internal account to suggest a relevant set of questions, of hypotheses to test. Secondly, the Indian account presented here may be local but it is not coeval with its subject: the paintings are of a later period than the buildings they depict. However, the architectural values which it embodies are not unique to the period when the paintings were made: profound and coherent, not transient or capricious, these values emerged from durable cultural habits. To take note of these values when approaching Mughal architecture, then, would be to develop what (adapting Baxandall) we might call a regional eye.

The English pictures may be useful to an English observer in so far as they can teach him much about how he sees, about which visual and conceptual habits he may need to break. The Indian pictures suggest what habits to adopt: they hint that when we analyse a Mughal building as an artificial, meaningful, ordered space, we are more nearly right, because we are more nearly approaching the cultural milieu which formed it.

[1] William Hodges, *Travels in India*, 2nd ed., London 1794, pp.iii-iv.

[2] Richard Payne Knight, *The Landscape: A Didactic Poem in Three Cantos*, London, 1794, p.14. See also: idem, *An Analytical Inquiry into the Principles of Taste*, 4th ed., London, 1808, pp.225-8; and, on the 'dethroning' of architecture, David Watkin, *The English Vision*, London, 1982, p.x.

[3] William Hodges, *A Dissertation on the Prototypes of Architecture: Hindoo, Moorish and Gothic*, London, 1787, p.1. See also: Hodges, 1794, pp.153-4.

[4] The ensuing comparison between English and Indian images of buildings is of a sort which I have previously sketched elsewhere: see G.H.R. Tillotson, 'The Paths of Glory: Representations of Sher Shah's Tomb', *Oriental Art*, vol.XXXVII no.1, 1991, pp.4-16; idem, 'Indian Architecture and the English Vision', *South Asian Studies*, vol.7, 1991, pp.59-74. The present chapter amplifies and extends the argument to the question of understanding architecture.

[5] See inter alia: Mildred Archer and Ronald Lightbown, *India Observed: India as Viewed by British Artists 1760-1860*, London, 1982; Pratapaditya Pal and Vidya Dehejia, *From Merchants to Emperors: British Artists and India 1757-1930*, London, 1986; Jagmohan Mahajan, *The Raj Landscape: British Views of Indian Cities*, South Godstone, 1988; Pheroza Godrej and Pauline Rohatgi, *Scenic Splendours: India through the Printed Image*, London, 1989: G.H.R. Tillotson, 'The Indian Picturesque: Images of India in British Landscape Painting, 1780-1880', *The Raj: India and the British 1600-1947*, ed. C.A. Bayly, London, 1990, pp.141-51.

[6] William Hodges, *Select Views in India*, no.18 (1787); the aquatint is based on a drawing in the Paul Mellon Collection (II/15) made in 1781. See: Isabel Stuebe, *The Life and Works of William Hodges*, New York, 1979, nos.328/9, p.249.

[7] Thomas and William Daniell, *Oriental Scenery*, vol.1, no.12 (1796).

[8] William Gilpin, *Three Essays: On Picturesque Beauty; on Picturesque Travel; and on Sketching Landscape*, London, 1792, p.7.

[9] Robert and James Adam, *Works in Architecture*, vol. 1 (1773), Introduction.

[10] Private collection; see Stuart Cary Welch, *Room for Wonder: Indian Painting during the British Period 1760-1880*, New York, 1985, p.134; I have followed Welch's dating and provenance for the work. See also: Pratapaditya Pal, *Romance of the Taj Mahal*, London, 1989, p.68.

[11] Welch, op.cit., p.134.

[12] One might cite, for example, the engraving by Brown after William Hodges, *A View of the Gate of the Tomb of the Emperor Akbar at Secundrii* (1786)—an illustration to Hodges, 1787 (see Stuebe, 1979, no.403, p.274).

[13] See Tillotson, 1991, pp.59, 61.

[14] See Raymond Head, *Catalogue of Paintings, Drawings, Engravings and Busts in the Collection of the Royal Asiatic Society*, London, 1991, no.017.004, p.70.

[15] Also in the collection of the Royal Asiatic Society (no.056.001) is a large painting on cloth, depicting Jahangir's tomb at Lahore, which shares many characteristics with the contemporary painting of Akbar's tomb (Fig.3): the focal tomb around which we walk is shown in perspective, the meaningfully planned garden is shown in plan, the screening gates are shown in elevation, and the boundary wall defines the picture's edge. See Head, op.cit., p.148 and pl.XXI.

[16] Hodges, *Select Views*; engraved titles to plates 18 and 13 (1787, 1786).

[17] One example is in the India Office Library and Records (WD 707), dated 1794.

[18] Mildred Archer, *Indian Architecture and the British*, Middlesex, 1968, p.39; idem, *Company Drawings in the India Office Library,* London, 1972, p.167.

[19] There are substantial collections in both the India Office Library and Records and the Victoria and Albert Museum, London; the current study is based on these, and on smaller groups in the Royal Asiatic Society and the British Architectural Library Drawings Collection (RIBA), London.

[20] IOLR Add Or 922; see Archer, 1972, p.172.

[21] A comparison might be made with the aquatint by Thomas and William Daniell, *The Taje Mahel, Agra, Taken in the Garden,* 1801.

[22] For another example, see RIBA F3/9.4.

[23] IOLR Add Or 933; see Archer, 1972, p.173.

[24] IOLR Add Or 1799; see Archer, 1972, p.183.

[25] IOLR Add Or 1800; see Archer, 1972, pp.183-4.

[26] IOLR Add Or 1806; see Archer, 1972, p.184.

[27] Thomas and William Daniell, Oriental Scenery, Vol.1, no.23 (1797).

[28] Archer, 1968, p.45; idem, 1972, p.168; idem, *Company Paintings: Indian Paintings of the British Period*, London, 1992, p.129.

[29] An example is IOLR MSS Eur.D.95 fol.65; see Tillotson, 1991, fig.16.

[30] See Head, op.cit., no.034.016, p.102.

[31] IOLR Add Or 1809; see Archer,1972, p.184.

[32] For example, IOLR Add Or 1133 and 1134 are based closely on Hodges, *Select Views,* nos.12 and 11; see Archer, 1972, pp.78-9.

[33] Stefan Collini, ed., *Interpretation and Overinterpretation*, Cambridge, 1992, p.25.

Chapter Four

INDIA'S VISUAL NARRATIVES:
THE DOMINANCE OF SPACE OVER TIME

Vidya Dehejia

While Western culture and Western scholarship have always given a
place of importance to chronology and the temporal sequence of events,
South Asianists are familiar with the complaint, even the accusation,
that India and Indians have never displayed a sense of history.[1] My
studies on the visual narratives of India, conducted especially in a
Buddhist context, would seem to confirm this widespread
generalisation. Artists telling stories, whether in the medium of stone
reliefs, terracotta panels or painted murals, generally gave lesser
importance to the element of time. Frequently, they emphasised
topographical location or geographical space at the expense of temporal
progression. This chapter analyses the visual artistic evidence and
raises queries as to why the element of time is relegated to a lesser
status.

Narrative, as Roland Barthes so aptly phrased it, is a human
universal; it is transnational, transcultural, transhistorical.[2] For a period
of around 600 years from the first century B.C.E. to 500 C.E., narrative
expressed itself fully and vibrantly in India in the context of Buddhist
art. It was the favourite choice of artists and patrons decorating the
numerous Buddhist monastic establishments that were built across the
country. At the centre of such complexes stood a stupa that housed a
portion of the relics of the Buddha. These sacred mounds that evoked
the presence of the Buddha were surrounded by railings and gateways
that were abundantly decorated with relief sculpture that was largely
narrative in character, and occasionally the mound itself was thus
adorned. The favourite themes were events from the Buddha's historic
life as Prince Siddhartha, and from his numerous previous births
(*jatakas*), often in animal form. Studies of Buddhist narrative have
examined the material either from the point of view of style and
chronology, or from the Buddhological and iconographical angle. My
studies of narrative focus instead on the neglected aspect of the
structure of narrative. The importance of narrative structure is self-
apparent in the field of literature where it is quite obvious that the same

story may be presented utilising different structures; for instance, it may be narrated as a poem or a drama or a novel. A narrative may be structured to commence in *medias res* with a climactic event after which it returns to the start, or it may follow the more standard 'once upon a time' temporal sequence. A comparable range of structural variation exists in visual narratives as well.

My study of the structure of visual narratives has led me to propose the existence of seven different modes through which ancient artists conveyed stories to their viewers.[3] I am currently carrying this project forward into an examination of the treatment of painted narrative in Rajput manuscripts. In each of these areas, it is strikingly evident that artists, whether of the first century B.C.E. or of the seventeenth through nineteenth centuries C.E., treated the element of time as of secondary significance. Only two of seven modes of narrative presentation are concerned with clarifying temporal progression.

Reduced to its basic elements, a story revolves around actions that occur in space and unfold in time. For the artist, the three major components of narrative are the protagonists of a story, and the two elements of time and space. In portraying their actors, artists must decide how to represent the space or spaces within which the story occurs, and how to shape the time during which the story unfolds.

I shall start with a brief discussion of two narrative modes that clarify the passage of time, only to set them aside for the rest of this chapter. The first is the sequential mode in which artists presented multiple episodes from a story, repeating the figures of the protagonists, distinctly framing each episode, and placing framed episodes in a clear linear sequence. Framing devices are most often architectural entities, with pilasters being of frequent usage as in a panel from the Buddhist site of Nagarjunakonda (Fig.1). Moving from right to left, we see four episodes from the story of the Buddha's half-brother Nanda. A damaged unit which contained the first scenes of the legend is followed by Nanda's coerced induction into the order with his head-shaving ceremony. The third episode depicts the Buddha taking Nanda (the two flying figures) up to Indra's heaven to view the beauty of the nymphs and thereby divert him from his desire to abandon the order and return to his wife. The final unit presents Nanda, cured of his love-sick condition, being hailed by the townsfolk. At this site, the framing pilasters enclose a *mithuna* couple, and such pilaster-framed intervening units serve to punctuate individual episodes of sequential

4   3

Fig. 1   Sequential Narrative: The Story of Nanda; Nagarjunakonda (after
Dietrich Schlingloff)

narrative. The story reads clearly, either from right to left as in this
instance, or from left to right, and temporal progression is explicitly
presented. Sequential narrative is of restricted occurrence, however,
being dominant only in the art of the northwestern region of Gandhara.

The second mode in which temporal progression is presented with a
degree of clarity is continuous narrative, which differs from sequential
narrative primarily in the absence of framing devices. Here too,
multiple episodes are presented, and the protagonist is repeated;
however, consecutive episodes are presented within a single visual field
without dividers to distinguish one time frame from the next. While
temporal succession (and spatial movement) is clearly indicated, the
comprehension of continuous narrative requires an integrating effort of
mind and eye on the part of the viewer. Yet the passage of time is quite
clear once the principle of continuous narrative has been grasped. An
architrave from a Sanchi gateway uses the continuous mode with much
success to present the Great Departure of the Buddha, with the action
moving from left to right (Fig.2). To the left, the Buddha emerges on
horseback from the palace gates. The Buddha is not presented here in
anthropomorphic form; instead his presence on horseback is indicated
by an indexical sign of empty space sheltered by a parasol that is held
at an appropriate height above the horse. To depict temporal
progression as the Buddha rides away from the palace, the artist has
repeated the protagonist horse-and-rider three times. The completion of
the episode, when the Buddha dismounts from the horse, is indicated at
the far end by the parasol poised above footprints. The horse, now
placed contrary to the movement thus far and minus its parasol,

2 1

Fig. 2 Continuous Narrative: The Great Departure of the Buddha; Sanchi

indicates that the riderless horse is returning to the palace. While there are no framing devices to separate one episode from the next, the multiple appearances of the horse and rider indicate successive moments of time and space, and will be read as such by viewers accustomed to the conventions of continuous narration.

I move now to modes of narration in which temporal progression is either ignored or given secondary status. In monoscenic narrative, artists simply avoided the entire issue of time by extracting a single, easily recognisable episode from a story and presenting it to stimulate the viewers' recognition of the whole story. An artist at the Bharhut

stupa portrayed the single scene of Prince Vessantara's gift of the
auspicious white state elephant, an action that caused the king, his
father, to banish him. The viewer is presented with just three figures,
albeit unmistakable ones—the elephant, the brahmin who receives the
gift, and the prince pouring water to ratify the gift (Fig.3). In portraying
this prelude to the story, the artist left viewers to narrate the entire
legend to themselves and recall the importance of charity, the most
important of the Buddhist virtues. The monoscenic mode is of
extensive occurrence at early Indian sites, and a second instance from
Bharhut will demonstrate the manner in which use of this mode enabled
artists to bypass the problem of temporality. To portray the Kukkuta
jataka that speaks of a she-chat who tried to induce a cock to become
her mate with the intention of devouring him, a Bharhut artist merely
depicted the two animals, the one at the foot of a tree and the other
perched upon it, deciding that they were sufficiently distinctive to
enable identification of the story (Fig.4). Viewers must remind
themselves of the tale and recall its moral—the danger of succumbing
to sensual desires. By its choice of a single scene to recall the entire
story, the monoscenic mode effectively deflects, almost eliminates, the
need to portray the passage of time that is certainly a challenge for the
artist who must deal with a two-dimensional surface.

Monoscenic narration often adopts the static mode, especially when
artists wished to emphasise the supremacy, wisdom and glory of the
Buddha. In the static mode, the artist portrays the single, culminating
episode of a story, and thus presents the result of a narrative sequence,
or the situation immediately following its occurrence. Three instances
of the use of this static mode, that stand in a diachronic relationship,
may be seen on a Bharhut pillar (Fig.5). The lowest panel portrays the
miracle at Sravasti in which the Buddha caused a full-grown mango
tree to emerge instantly from a seed. The artist was not interested in the
sequence of events that led to the performance of the miracle; instead
we are presented with the aftermath of the miracle, when the mango
tree had already sprung up. The panel focuses on the supremacy of the
Buddha whose indexical presence is indicated by the parasol-sheltered
throne beneath the mango tree. Viewers must now move to the topmost
panel to follow the Buddha to the Trayastrimsa heavens to which he
ascended after the Sravasti miracle in order to preach to the gods. The
need to deal with the element of time is again dispensed with since the
artist merely portrays the actual preaching through the portrayal of a
parasol-sheltered throne beneath a tree surrounded by the gods. The
cycle concludes with the central panel which portrays the Buddha's

Fig. 3 Monoscenic Narrative: The Story of Vessantara; Bharhut

Fig. 4 Monoscenic Narrative: The Kukkuta *jataka*; Bharhut

descent from the heavens at Sankissa, accompanied by Indra and Brahma. Three ladders are seen at the right of the panel and the footprints at the top and bottom rungs of the central ladder are indexical traces of the Buddha's descent. The Buddha's presence amidst his

Fig. 5   Static Monoscenic Narrative, diachronic mode: Sravasti to Sankissa
cycle; Bharhut

Fig. 6 Gaya-Uruvela pillar; Sanchi

devotees after his descent is indicated to the left of the panel by the indexical sign of a seat beneath a garland-hung tree. It is curious that the artist used neither a direct top-to-bottom progression, nor one from bottom to top, to present the Sravasti to Sankissa Buddhological cycle. As we have seen, the viewer is required to start at the bottom, move to the top, and end at the centre. Possibly a geographical (or cosmological) logic is at work here. The artist may have felt that the heavens should be at the top of the pillar, the earth at the bottom, and the descent between.

Such lack of adherence to a logical temporal sequence is not exceptional; in fact, it is more the norm than the exception. It is evident, for instance, on the two adjacent faces of a pillar at Sanchi that portrays a series of incidents connected with the Gaya-Uruvilva miracles of the Buddha (Fig.6). The artist combined two episodes relating to the enlightenment with the series of later miracles connected with the conversion of the Kasyapas. To complete one face of the pillar before sculpting the adjoining face would be a logical way to proceed. But the Sanchi artist did not do this. The top two panels of the outer face present the enlightenment episodes; however, rather than continuing on the front face, the artist moved to the inner face to present three panels pertaining to the Kasyapa ascetics and their conversion. To complete the Kasyapa story, viewers must return to the front face to view the climactic miracle of walking on the waters; the lowest panel then portrays the Buddha with his new Kasyapa converts at the town of Rajagriha where they are met by King Bimbisara. One explanation for the artist's organisation could lie in the fact that the miracle of walking on the waters was regarded by the donor or the artist, or by both, as the most significant of the series. Rather than place it in its correct sequence, where it would have appeared at the top of the inner face and been viewed with difficulty, the artist placed it at easily readable eye-level on the front face where it would attract appropriate attention.

A Sanchi pillar devoted to the seven 'stations' that represent the seven weeks following the enlightenment likewise departs from the direct temporal presentation of the seven weeks. Reading from top to bottom, the inner face presents a prelude in the form of the *bodhi* tree of the first earthly Buddha Vipassi, followed by stations 4, 1a, 1b and 3; the front face carried stations 6, 7a, 7b and probably the missing 5 and 2 in its damaged lower segment. Such blatant disregard for the temporal sequence is curious. Perhaps the positioning of panel 7b at eye-level on the front face reflects the importance assigned to its portrayal of the Buddha's very first disciples, the merchants Trapussa and Bhallika. At the early Buddhist monastic site of Sanchi, the theme of conversion may have held special significance.

Synoptic narration, in which multiple episodes of a story are depicted within a single frame, with repeated depictions of the protagonist, makes no attempt at all to communicate temporal progression. There is no consistent or formal order of presentation with regard to the temporal sequence from one synoptic portrayal to the next; instead, totally arbitrary compositional schemes appear to be followed as will be evident from the two examples presented here.

A synoptic portrayal of the monkey story at Sanchi presents five episodes within a rectangular panel (Fig.7). The viewer's attention is likely to be caught by the river that curves across the panel, the six prominent foreground figures, and perhaps by the monkey straddling the panel at its very top; however, even knowing viewers must closely scrutinise the panel to read the story in its correct sequence. They will realise that the foreground figures are of little relevance to the action, and that the entire section to the far side of the river is marginal to the tale which actually unfolds in about a quarter of the panel's space. Behind the foreground figures, a monarch arrives on horseback, while roughly at the centre of the panel is the half-hidden figure of an archer, bending backwards as he shoots his arrow upwards. At the top is a monkey stretched out to form a bridge across the river below, and we may surmise that his fellow monkeys are escaping to the safety of the opposite bank. Below the monkey two men hold a stretcher to indicate the fall of the monkey (not actually depicted), while to the left are seated figures of monkey and monarch to signify the monkey's sermon to the king on the importance of attending to the welfare of his followers. The artist has certainly not facilitated the reading of the tale in the coherent manner presented here. However, a spatial structure underlies his presentation, with emphasis on the left bank of the river where the action occurs and the danger lies, while the safe environment lies on the opposite bank.

A second instance of synoptic narrative, in a medallion from Amaravati which portrays the story of elephant Chaddanta in seven scenes, presents even fewer clues to its decipherment (Fig.8). The centre of the medallion is 'dead' space, and the story commences to the right of the central zone with Chaddanta in the forest with his identifying regal parasol held above him (1). Three scenes unfold in the lower zone that is treated as a lotus-filled lake. First, Chaddanta

Fig. 7 Synoptic Narrative: The monkey *jataka*; Sanchi

presents a lotus to his chief queen, Maha-subhadda (2); to the left his
offended and jealous junior queen, Culla-subhadda, leaves the pond (3)
and lies down to die praying for revenge in a future birth (4). The story
now moves to the upper zone where a hunter concealed in a pit (sent by
Culla-subhadda reborn as queen of Benares) aims his arrow at the

Fig. 8 Synoptic Narrative: The story of the elephant Chaddanta; Amaravati

unsuspecting Chaddanta (5). To the left, Chaddanta acquiesces as the hunter saws off the tusks desired by the queen (6), while at the very top of the medallion, the hunter departs with the tusks.

The manner in which viewers must approach synoptic narrative in order to unravel the time sequence is almost the opposite of the way in which one hears or reads a story. Rather than putting elements together to make a whole, the whole is presented to viewers who must take it apart in order to make it intelligible. The articulation of temporal succession was evidently of little consequence to the artists. It is interesting to ponder over the reasons for this subversion of the element of time. One cannot but wonder if there is any underlying cultural explanation for its popularity. The fact that time, in India, is considered to be cyclical rather than linear may possibly have something to do with its apparent disregard in much of visual narration. At the same time, one wonders if the ancient artists would have been amused, or perhaps peeved, if asked why they had not presented temporal progression more explicitly!

The mode of conflated narrative which is complementary to the synoptic mode with which it shares several features, employs the characteristic overlapping mode of presentation that subverts temporal progression even further. Instead of repeating the figure of the protagonist from scene to scene within the multiple episodes of a story, there is a conflation of that figure. A typical example of conflated narrative is the Gandharan portrayal of the Dipankara *jataka* (Fig.9), in which brahmin Sumedha worships Dipankara Buddha (whose figure is conflated) who predicts his future birth as Buddha Gautama. The enlarged figure of Dipankara is placed in the right half of the panel. At the extreme left, Sumedha buys lotuses; he then throws them at Dipankara (they remain suspended around his head), spreads out his long hair upon the muddy ground for the Buddha to step up, and rises up into the air upon hearing Dipankara's pronouncement. The single large figure of Dipankara is to be read as receiving the lotuses, perceiving Sumedha's hair spread out before him, and making the pronouncement of the future birth, and thus participating in three scenes in which Sumedha is portrayed three times. In such instances of conflation, one may view the choice of the mode as intended to convey the Buddha's transcendence over both space and time. The single image of Dipankara is the visual equivalent, spatially, to three Sumedhas; and the single image possesses the ability to participate in more than one

Fig. 9 Conflated Narrative: The story of Dipankara; Gandhara

Fig. 10 Conflated Narrative: The Quail *jataka*; Bharhut

moment of time. In such cases, it may be possible to view the use of conflation as reflecting the values, vis-à-vis its founder, that is central to any system of religious beliefs.

A different explanation must be found for the use of conflation in the quail *jataka* story, in which the quail (who is not the Buddha in a previous life) is placed on a tree to the right of centre, and a set of six scenes that unfold around her all refer to her single presence (Fig.10). The lower half of the medallion portrays two elephants to represent the herd of the *bodhisattva* elephant to whom the quail appealed, and who peaceably walked past her nest on the ground, in which were baby quails too young to fly. Above is the rogue elephant who followed shortly thereafter; ignoring the quail's appeal, he deliberately trampled

upon the nest that is seen to the left at the point where the medallion is
damaged. Swearing revenge, the quail sought help from three friends, a
crow, a fruit-fly and a frog, in order to destroy the elephant. The
medallion contains a second instance of conflation in the figure of the
rogue elephant who is part of three successive scenes, all of which refer
to a single image. The same elephant who crushes the nest of baby
quails, has his eyes pecked out by a crow, and eggs laid in the wound
by the fruit-fly. The croaking frog at the top of the medallion brings
about the elephant's death. Expecting to find water, the blinded
elephant plunges to his death; here, the artist provides a second image
of the elephant falling over the cliff. The explanation for the use of
conflation in this medallion, and the consequent compression and
undermining of time, is curious. The centralised positioning of the
single image of the quail may have been dictated by compositional
considerations in which she provided a logical point of reference. When
a single character participates in a number of episodes, the artist could
avoid needless repetition by placing that character in a central location.

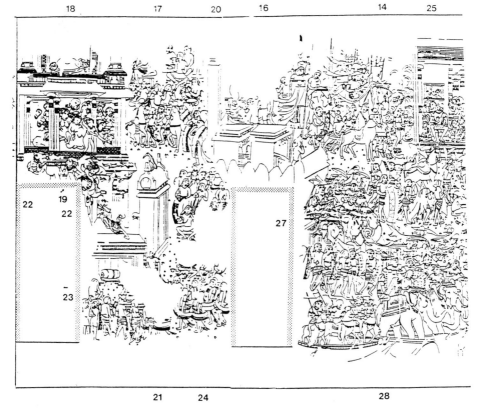

Fig. 11   Narrative Network: Simhala story; Cave 17, Ajanta (after Dieter
Schlingloff)

The conflation of the figure of the rogue elephant, however, is somewhat strange unless the device was adopted merely due to shortage of space. Whatever the exact nature of the explanation, the artist was undoubtedly making certain deliberate choices.

The mode of narration that most blatantly ignores the temporal sequence is the narrative network that is seen at its most expressive in the fifth-century murals decorating the caves at Ajanta. Frequently, the entire side walls of *viharas*, interrupted by doorways into the cells for monks, are given over to the depiction of a single narrative, resulting in presentations of labyrinthine complexity. Interlaced sequences meander their way across the walls in such a manner that several Ajanta murals have long defied identification. Few clues exist as to where a particular network might commence, nor as to where it might end. Some start in the centre, others at left or right, and there is no predictability in their movement.

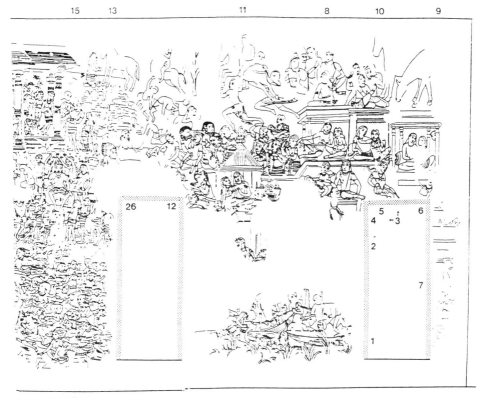

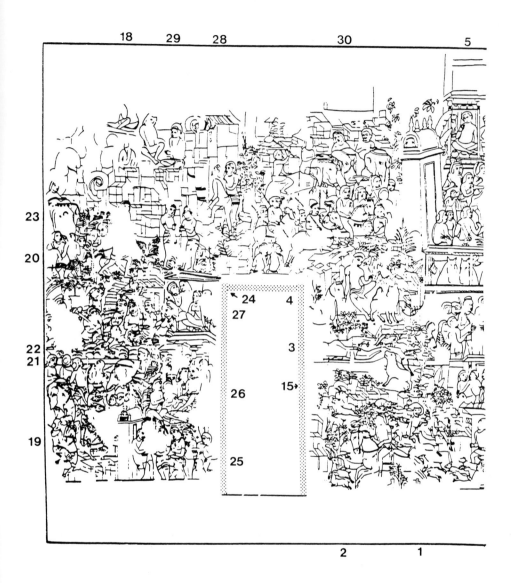

Fig. 12 Narrative Network: Saudasa-Sutasoma story; Cave 17, Ajanta (after Dieter Sclingloff)

An extensive network on the right wall of cave 17, that occupies a space 45 feet across and 15 feet from floor to ceiling (Fig.11), tells the story of merchant Simhala in a total of 29 scenes that contain numerous repetitions of the figure of the protagonist. The action moves in seemingly unpredictable fashion, commencing at the lower right and moving upwards, then working its way across the upper segment to the left where it meanders downwards, finally culminating in the central space. Within each of these three segments—right, left and centre—the

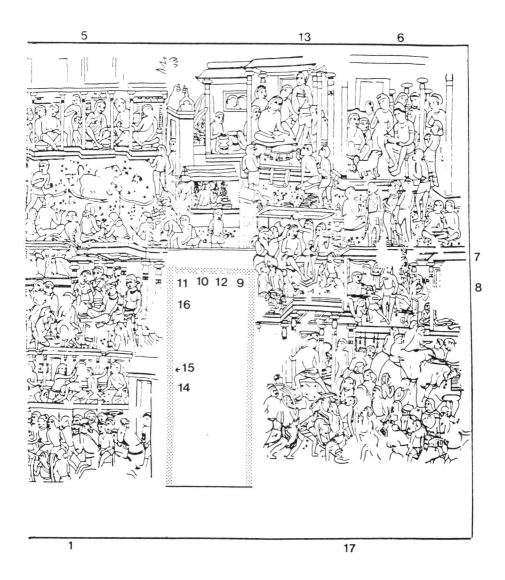

action moves in cross-cross fashion and no specific pattern emerges. In fact, one is confronted with a network of movement in space and time. Yet a closer analysis indicates that the story may be viewed basically in terms of geographical or topographical space. The right third of the narrative takes place on the witches' island; the left third is the palace of the king; while the central space that contains the conclusion of the story, as well as certain earlier episodes, appears to be space associated with Simhala. Its upper area portrays Simhala's home, its central zone his coronation, and its lower area his climactic confrontation with the witches.

The left rear wall of cave 17 contains a smaller network that occupies only 20 feet of space, and portrays the story of Sutasoma and Saudasa in a total of 30 scenes (Fig.12). The story commences at the lower centre, moves to the right segment, then jumps across to the left segment, and concludes in the upper centre of the wall space. Again a geographical and spatial logic is evident in the system. The central segment contains the prelude to the story and relates to King Sudasa of Benares and the lioness with whom he mated to produce the child Saudasa. The space to the right belongs to Saudasa and his town of Benares; it depicts his childhood and youth and his gradual transformation into a consumer of human flesh. Attacked by his own army, he flees his town. The space to the left represents Prince Sutasoma's town of Hastinapura. Captured by man-eating Saudasa, Sutasoma appeals to him for release for just as long as it would take him to keep his promise to a brahmin. When he returns in face of certain death, Saudasa is overwhelmed and accepts him as teacher. The peaceful ending to the tale is seen to the upper left of the central space.

The network that is painted along a 15-foot span of the left wall of cave 16 presents the conversion of Buddha's half-brother Nanda (Fig.13). The story commences in the lower central area and concludes

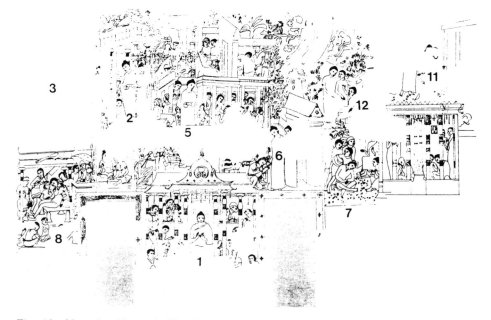

Fig. 13   Narrative Network: Nanda story; Cave 16, Ajanta (after Diter Schlingloff)

in the upper right segment; within this area the narrative moves freely with no apparent pattern until, again, the spatial arrangement is considered. The left space is devoted to the worldly life of pleasure and portrays Nanda's home; the right segment depicts scenes in the monastery; while the broad central segment is devoted to scenes in the town of Kapilavastu in which, generally, the Buddha is the central figure.

The entire right wall of cave 16, some 40 feet in length, is given over to a depiction of the pre-enlightenment life of the Buddha (Fig.14). Commencing with the Buddha's decision in the Tushita heavens to descend to earth, the mural concludes with him proceeding towards the deer park at Sarnath, having omitted the scene of the enlightenment, but giving prominence to Sujata's offering of rice pudding. Using the narrative network, the artist portrayed a total of 31 scenes which are not arranged according to their temporal sequence. Scene 23 of the aftermath of the four drives occurs at the left extreme of the wall; scene 24, portraying the sleeping Yashodara and the decision to leave home, appears at the right extreme of the same wall, adjoining the earlier episode of his marriage. A spatial logic that ignores the temporal sequence is at work in this apparently random placing. The right segment of the mural portrays all episodes which occurred within the palace at Kapilavastu; thus, the interpretation of Queen Maya's dream (3), the marriage of Siddhartha and Yashodara (20), and the prince surrounded by the sleeping women (24), are found side by side, although the three episodes are separated by considerable time-spans. The central segment of the wall portrays a number of momentous episodes that occurred outside the walls of Kapilavastu, such as the entire series of scenes connected with the birth of the Buddha, his visit to the temple, and his great feat of archery. The left segment contains scenes that occurred far from Kapilavastu and generally pertain to the Buddha's pursuit of Buddha-hood; these include his first meditation, his four drives, his encounters with various holy men, his meeting with King Bimbisara, and Sujata's offering. It is this geographical placement that accounts for scene 24 (Buddha leaving the sleeping Yashodara) being placed at the extreme right of the narrative, while scenes 21-23 (outside the palace, prior to the renunciation) and scenes 25-31 (after the departure) are at the opposite end.

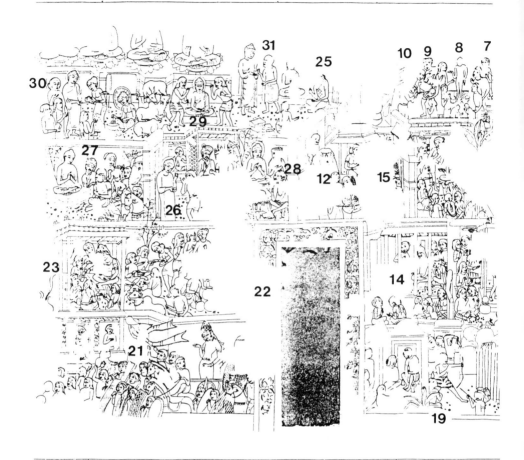

Fig. 14 Narrative Network: Pre-enlightenment life of Buddha; Cave 15, Ajanta
(after Dieter Schlingloff)

It is intriguing to consider if it is possible to see anything in common
between the complex visual narrative networks and the stream of
consciousness apparent in novels like James Joyce's *Ulysses* where a
reader can go 50 pages without finding punctuation. What was Joyce's,
or for that matter Gabriel Marquez's, intention in the use of such a
method? And more importantly, what is the effect of such a narrative
presentation upon its audience? Verbally, one feels submerged in the
events, surrounded by the characters, and practically one of the
performers. Visually, the effect is strikingly similar. Viewers are not
given the choice of stepping away at the end of one episode; before
they realise it, they have already entered into the one following. The
viewer becomes a participant in the narrative.

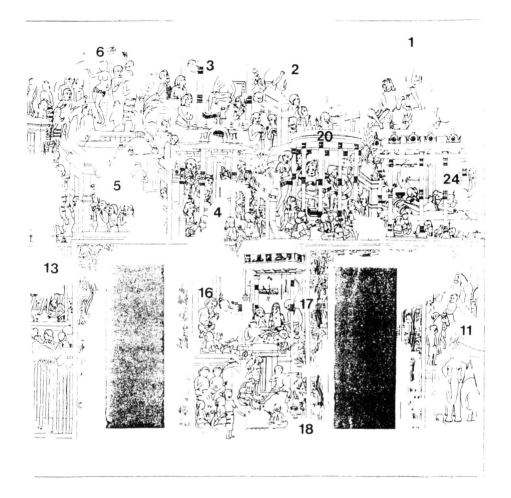

It is interesting to speculate on whether the lesser importance assigned to the element of time in India's visual narratives is partially due to the system followed by much of its literary narrative in which plots contain sub-plots, and stories are contained within stories. For instance, in the compendium of animal tales and fables known as *Hitopadesa*, the story-line of each of its four books is interrupted so often by the narration of other tales, that listeners and readers have often forgotten the original story and have certainly lost track of its time-sequence. Its first section titled 'Acquisition of Friends' is basically the story of the friendship that developed between a crow, a mouse, a tortoise and a deer, but its narration is interrupted by the presentation of six other stories,[4] that make it difficult to keep track of the temporal and causal sequence of the main legend. This system of literary narrative, oral and written, was a standard pattern in India, and the great *Mahabharata* epic, for instance, proceeds along similar principles. Popular oral tellings and dramatised versions of various works take great satisfaction in presenting their numerous sub-plots. Versions staged in villages and small towns often introduce a character whose sole purpose is to ensure that the action is frozen in order to introduce a sub-plot; frequently such a character enlists the support of the audience in urging the narration of sub-stories.

This literary model of pan-Indian occurrence is also found in a specifically Buddhist context. In the *Mahavastu*, the very life-story of the Buddha is interrupted at regular intervals by none other than the Buddha himself who narrates legends of his previous lives.[5] In the later Pali *jataka* collection too, stories are stalled on occasion in order to narrate another tale.[6] Belonging to a milieu in which stories, written, oral or dramatic, rarely proceeded in a direct and uninterrupted fashion, ancient sculptors and painters may have attached little consequence to an ordered presentation of temporality in their visual narratives.

The principle of topographical location evident in Ajanta's narrative networks, or the 'primacy of place over time',[7] is seen to be the guiding principle in the large painted scrolls of the contemporary Rajasthani *Pabuji-ka-pur* tradition. John D. Smith's study indicates that the central space of a 15-foot-long *par* is occupied by the court of the protagonist, Pabuji. The left and right extremes represent the territories of his chief enemies, while the space between is occupied by the courts of various neighbours and allies. Figure 15 reproduces a marginally altered

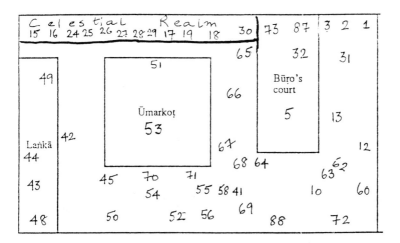

Fig. 15 Schematic 'map' of *Pabuji-ki-par* (after John D. Smith)

version of his schematic map of a *par*, upon which I have superimposed numbers corresponding to the hundred scenes into which Smith divides the story. Episodes 10 and 11 that follow each other in the temporal unravelling of this extensive narrative are not located next to each other as they would be if the artist had used the system of continuous narration, or if the temporal sequence held significance for him. Instead, number 10 is to the left of Pabuji's court while number 11 is to the far right. Such a placement is dictated by the geographical location of scene 10 in Patan, to the west, and the succeeding scene 11 in Pushkar, to the east. Equally, episodes placed next to each other may have no temporal connection; their contiguous placement merely reflects their occurrence in the same geographical space. Scene 46 (news from Lanka presented to Pabuji), scene 59 (wedding proposal presented to Pabuji), and scene 100 (enemy's severed head presented at Pabuji's court) are temporally separated by considerable spans of time; their adjacent placement reflects the fact that each occurred at the identical location of Pabuji's court. It is interesting to note that the upper border of the *par* appears to represent celestial space, being occupied by the various deities invoked during the course of the story; their numbering reflects their temporal sequence in the legend of Pabuji. While geographical space is tightly organised in the *par* tradition, Ajanta's networks, while making use of this principle, are less strictly regulated by it. Within the three geographical areas of each of Ajanta's networks, we find an amazing convolution of movement in space and time.

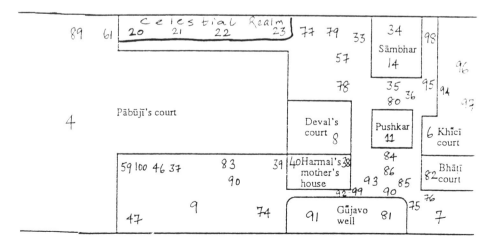

It is pertinent to raise the issue of whether identification of seven modes of visual narration merely provides modern scholars with a useful tool, or whether such modes were ancient indigenous distinctions. No texts survive that advise artists on modes of presenting narratives; one might remark that such evidence is equally lacking in the case of Egyptian, Roman, Etruscan or Christian narratives. On the other hand, it is clear that artistic choices were being made. One artist at the site of Bharhut adopted the monoscenic mode to present the Vessantara *jataka*, while a second chose sequential narrative for the same *jataka*. Two Sanchi sculptors opted for the monoscenic mode to portray the Chaddanta story, while a third decided on continuous narrative for that popular elephant story. Once we acknowledge that ancient artists were making deliberate decisions on the manner in which they wished to communicate their message, it seems necessary to assume the existence of a theoretical framework. The visual evidence provided by artistic material, which is surely as revelatory as textual sources,[8] seems to speak for itself; it seems that we must admit the existence, in ancient India, of a sophisticated concept of visual narration.

In concluding, a few brief comments may be made on the issue of viewer-response. In the case of the narrative network, for instance, one might ask whether the viewer was actually intended to unravel the labyrinthine sequences and experience the tale in its correct temporal order? Certainly it would have required 'strong eyes, great persistence and an excellent retentive memory'[9] to do so, even if the viewer was aided by a monk familiar with the tale who may have acted as a spiritual guide.[10] It is also intriguing to speculate on the factors that may have governed the choice of narratives. Certainly gifts were linked with donors in rather complex ways. Using the Vessantara story as a case in point, one could postulate that if it were portrayed by order of the monastic community, its aim may have been to present an exemplary example to wealthy pilgrims hoping to induce them to make substantial donations. On the other hand, if the story was the donor's choice, the intention may have been to set up a parallel between the donor's own gifting and that of Vessantara.

A final reflection is that certain narratives were probably placed upon monuments because they needed to be there for the value of the monument itself, rather than for reading by monks, pilgrims or patrons. It is likely that carved or painted guardians were placed at entrances to stupas and monasteries because such figures were considered propitious. Probably, it was deemed equally beneficial for these sacred monuments to be decorated with *jataka* tales and life-scenes of the Buddha. When one contemplates the many narratives that are placed beyond the reach of easy observation by pilgrim, monk or patron, it seems that this factor may not be discounted. A case in point is provided by the plaques decorating the six inaccessible roof terraces of the Ananda temple at Pagan in Burma. In the absence of stairwells, neither pilgrims nor monks could view the complete set of 537 *jataka* plaques adorning the three lower terraces, nor the 375 plaques portraying the last ten *jatakas* placed against the three upper terraces. Clearly, the placement of these narratives was not motivated by the aspect of viewing; rather, in the Burmese Buddhist scenario, it is apparent that *jatakas* were deemed a necessary efficacious part of the decoration. One may cite also a practice of comparable significance in the oral narration of the Hindu epic *Ramayana* at certain ritual occasions in India. Instead of serving as a focus in itself, the recitation serves as a background chant that is scarcely attended to in any active fashion. Yet the narration is a part of the ceremonial and necessary to add to its validity and significance.[11] It is likely that the visual narratives that form the subject of this study were intended for a diverse audience, and that an entire range of factors functioned in complex combinations to result in the rich narrative decoration of the early Buddhist monuments of India.

---

[1] In a recent conference convened at Columbia University, a scholar of Portuguese history went to the extent of maintaining that without the Portuguese and the British, India would never have developed a sense of chronology or history!

[2] Roland Barthes, 'Introduction to the Structural Analysis of Narratives', in *Image—Music—Text*, essays selected and translated by Stephen Heath, London, 1977, p.79.

[3] Vidya Dehejia, 'On Modes of Visual Narrative in Eary Buddhist Art', *Art Bulletin*, September 1990, pp.372-92.

[4] A pigeon-king who is a minor participant in the main story narrates story 1; the mouse relates story 2 but is himself interrupted by one of story 2's characters narrating story 3. Having found our way back to the mouse, the story moves on but is put on hold by the mouse who tells story 4. The main story inches along; the tortoise relates story 5; the mouse brings in story 6; and finally the main legend comes to a conclusion.

[5] Remarking that a particular situation had occurred previously, the Buddha repeatedly narrates stories of previous lives. Thus at the great departure, the Buddha narrates the legend of the courtesan Syama to illustrate that he had left Yasodhara on previous occasions (J.J. Jones, *The Mahavastu*, London, 1949-1956, 161ff.) When King Suddhodhana refuses to believe that his son has died of excessive penance, the Buddha narrates the Syama *jataka* to illustrate that on a previous occasion too, Suddhodhana had refused to believe his son dead (ibid., 199 ff.). To illustrate that he had previously fallen into the hands of Mara but had been able to escape, the Buddha narrates a tortoise *jataka* (ibid., 232ff.).

[6] See E.B. Cowell, *The Jataka or Stories of the Buddha's Former Births* (London, 1877-1896). For instance, the *Mahsa-panada jataka* (no.264) is interrupted by the story of Surici which is also given independently as *jataka* 489. Similarly, the Mittavinda *jataka* (no.369) is in fact a fragment of *jataka* 41. Other examples of such a practice exist.

[7] John D. Smith, *The Epic of Pabuji: a study, transcription and translation* (Cambridge, 1991), p.57.

[8] Gergory Schopen has eloquently and convincingly argued against the primacy of textual versus archaeological material in the study of the Buddhist religion. See his 'Archaeology and Protestant suppositions in the study of Indian Buddhism', *History of Religions* 31, 1 (August 1991), pp.1-23.

[9] Richard Brilliant, *Visual Narratives: storytelling Roman and Etruscan art*, Ithaca, 1984, p.63.

[10] A variety of alternate possibilities exists; for a complete discussion see my forthcoming 'Discourses in early Buddhist art: visual narratives of India'.

[11] I am indebted to V. Narayana Rao (verbal communication) for this observation.

Chapter Five

FORM, TRANSFORMATION AND MEANING IN INDIAN TEMPLE ARCHITECTURE

Adam Hardy

> Verily, truth is sight. Therefore if two people should come disputing, saying 'I have seen', 'I have heard', we should trust the one who says, 'I have seen'. (Bṛhad-āraṇyaka Upaniṣad 5.14.4.[2].)[1]

This Upanishadic wisdom should be heeded by people who rush to documents before using their eyes. An understanding of the forms of Indian temples, the way these forms evolve, and their meaning depends upon seeing the architecture in the right way.[2]

Art historians now tend to distrust grand historical schemes, whether (synchronic) attempts to explain the creations of a given time in terms of a world-view or of a Spirit of the Age, or (diachronic) explanations of how art forms develop.[3] Attempts to attribute meanings to forms also tend to meet with the same kind of scepticism, often deservedly.[4] Here, however, if 'truth is sight', it can be seen that Indian temple architecture does follow a kind of 'grand scheme', both synchronic and diachronic, and also concerning meaning. The kind of pattern underlying the complex rhythmic compositions of individual temples can also be found in the evolutionary transformations that architectural forms undergo in the course of a tradition. This pattern is congruent with archetypal ideas in Indian thought, to the extent that the architecture can be said to have an intrinsic meaning. Formal structure and meaning are both rooted in a world-view, which the temples, almost by definition, must reflect, being conceived as microcosms or images of the universe.

Briefly stated, the 'pattern' in question is a dynamic one of centrifugal growth, clearly and unambiguously represented, through architectural means. In mature varieties of Hindu temple, the shrine proper (called *vimāna* in Drāviḍa or 'southern' temple architecture, *mūlaprāsāda* in the Nāgara or 'northern' context) is invested with a sense of movement that appears to originate at the finial, or at an infinitesimal point above its tip, continuing downwards, and outwards from the vertical axis of the shrine, radiating all around, but especially in the four cardinal directions (Fig.1). As the forms evolve downwards,

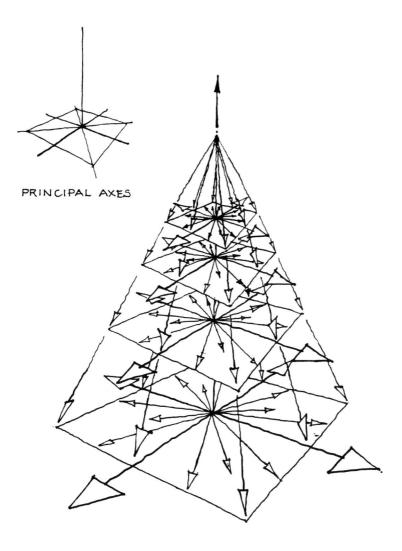

PRINCIPAL AXES

PRINCIPAL DIRECTIONS OF MOVEMENT

Fig. 1 Axes and Movement in a Vimana or Mulaprasada

the summit recedes and the whole monument grows. Two kinds of movement underlie the process: emergence and expansion. As the temple architecture portrays, these are indivisible stages in a single pattern of emanation and growth, which continues without pause into decay, as forms fall apart and re-merge into undifferentiation. Like its origin, the destination of this movement is beyond the visible limits of the monument, but it is sensed in the dissolution of the parts, which begins in their very act of emergence.

Through its dynamic structure a *vimāna* or a *mūlaprāsāda* becomes a symbol of manifestation: of the enshrined god and its various aspects, and in another sense, of the universe.[5] Manifestation is to be understood not as a single event but a continuous process—not fixed cosmology but ceaseless cosmogony. Such clear analogies can be drawn between the patterns of form and metaphysical ideas about manifestation, recurrent in Indian thought, that the ideas can be said to be embodied.

The focus of this chapter, as of this volume, will be the question of method, of how buildings of another age and culture can be properly understood, of the means by which it can be shown that a particular way of looking at a particular kind of architecture is valid. But it is first necessary to explain the matter with which the method is concerned, by looking at Indian temples in terms of their formal composition and evolution, and of their meaning.

Composition

Compositional structure in Indian temples is not entirely abstract, divorced from imagery. Perhaps more than any other architecture, that of Indian temples, notwithstanding a process of abstraction which takes place, is representational, made up of images. Stone or brick structures are composed of imagery derived from wooden buildings roofed with thatch, translated into a language of masonry. All but the most basic forms of temple are essentially composite, composed of interconnected aedicules, that is, of multiple representations of shrines or divine abodes.[6] Just as a divinity has many aspects, a great house for the god is made up of a collection of little houses, of various kinds and at various levels of order, from primary components to sculpture-sheltering niches. The compositional structure of the temples, with its centrifugal dynamism, is largely a matter of patterns of interrelation between the 'aedicular components'.

A further block to understanding has been the tendency to see exterior composition of temples as 'surface decoration', and therefore to imagine that it is a kind of relief, conceived two-dimensionally. It has even been referred to as 'decorative veneer' as if it were something stuck on. This is very far from the case. An important principle is 'embeddedness', the rendering of three-dimensionally conceived forms as if partly subsumed in, partly emerged from, their background. This way of thinking perhaps developed through the early importance of carving in solid rock, from which the architectural and sculptural forms emerged as they were hewn from the cliff face. In Indian temple architecture embeddedness is generally found in conjunction with 'enshrinement', the housing of something in a shrine or shrine-image. It is in shrine-images that the embedded forms, whether divine images or lesser shrine-images, are embedded. Enshrinement, of course, is the first purpose of the temple itself, developed into the multiple enshrinement of a multi-aedicular structure.

A particular kind of sequential chain dependent upon embeddedness and enshrinement, is characteristic in the temple dynamics, whereby one form gives birth to another, which in turn puts forth another, and so on; a pattern closely paralleled by theological/cosmological hierarchies which will be discussed presently. The form that is farthest forward, most exposed, appears as the latest emanation, lowest in the hierarchy.

In a Drāviḍa *vimāna* the primary shrine-images, surrounding the tiers (*talas*) of the pyramidal structure, represent *alpa vimāna*: two-storey shrines crowned, most often, by upper pavilions in the form of domed *kūṭas* or barrel-roofed *śālās*. Fig.2a shows the embedded aedicules in a simple of Drāviḍa *vimāna*, consisting, in the first *tala*, of central '*śālā*-aedicules' and corner '*kūṭa*-aedicules', with an 'upper temple' in the form of a more squat variety of *alpa vimāna*.

By contrast, the Latina form of Nāgara *mūlaprāsāda* appears as a single unit, although it may contain minor aedicules within its radiating segments. In Fig.2b is shown a simple version of the Śekhari mode, clearly composite, with the Latina *śikhara* as a basic compositional element, either by itself or capping a *kūṭastambha*, a *śikhara*-topped pillar form.

Having grasped the nature of the basic components and the ways in which they fit together, we may look at the patterns of interrelation between them. The representation of movement that I have described is achieved through a number of architectural means illustrated in Fig.3, two or more of which are often used together, reinforcing one another:

a)   Projection. Projection (throwing forward) of an embedded form suggests emergence, particularly if there is a sense of direction—forwards, sideways or diagonal.

b)   Staggering. Multiple projections create staggering, with offsets or step-like serrations. The stepped bulging of a surface, growing out in stages, suggests expansion (as in the staggered or expanding square plan). Multiple projection in conjunction with multiple embeddedness or interpenetration can convey a multiple emanation, either unidirectional, like the unfolding of a telescope, or in four or more

alpa vimāna

pañjara-
aedicule
(as wall-shrine)

śālā-aedicule

kūṭa-aedicule

a. DRĀVIDA VIMĀNA

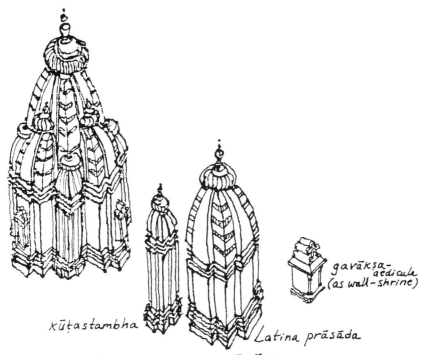

kūṭastambha

Latina prāsāda

gavākṣa-
aedicule
(as wall-shrine)

b. NĀGARA (ŚEKHARI) MULAPRĀSĀDA

Fig 2 Embedded Aedicular Components

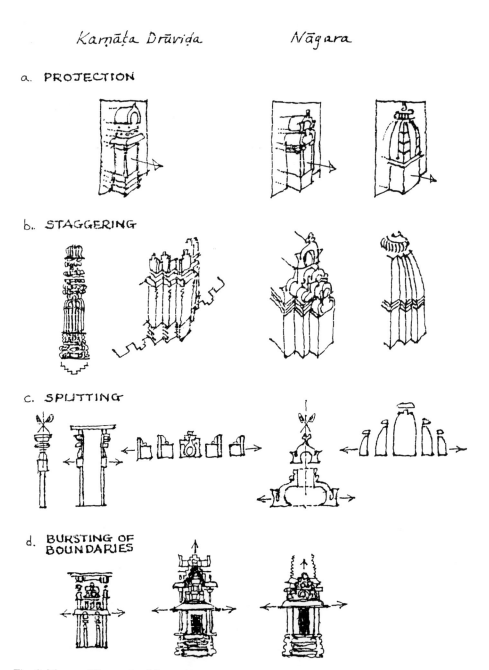

Fig. 3 Means of Expressing Movement

directions. Closely serrated edges may create the impression that a form is vibrating, as if with inner energy.

c)   Splitting. Where an element is represented as having split down the middle, the two halves having moved apart, there is a sense that the

Karṇāṭa Drāviḍa   *Nāgara*

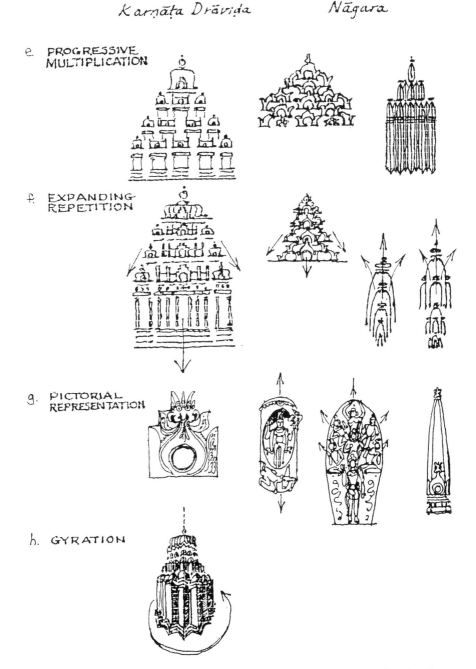

e. PROGRESSIVE MULTIPLICATION

f. EXPANDING REPETITION

g. PICTORIAL REPRESENTATION

h. GYRATION

space contained by the element expands on both sides. Another form revealed between a split pair will appear to emerge from the void.

d) Bursting of boundaries. A sense of the emergence and expansion of an enshrined form will be all the stronger if projection is accompanied by a penetration or overlap of the surrounding frame.

e) Progressive multiplication. A transformation from unity to multiplicity is expressed by an expanding, proliferating pattern. A single element begins a sequence of rows in which the number of elements progressively increases.

f) Expanding repetition. In a rhythmic series, the elements are all similar, but get progressively bigger.

g) Pictorial representation. While I would argue that all these means of conveying movement are representational, some kinds of depiction in a direct, pictorial way, are unquestionably so, as when a *nāsī* (horseshoe arch) or *tōraṇa* (archway) is shown pouring out of the jaws of a monster-finial. A purely sculptural rather than architectural example of pictorially-represented emergence and expansion is the widespread image of the *liṅgodbhava* myth, in which Śiva appears and grows from an orifice in the side of the expanding *liṅga*, while Brahmā (in bird form) and Viṣṇu (in boar form) strive vainly to catch up with its ever-receding ends. Such an image is not made to be seen in isolation from its architectural setting, and in this context can enhance the dynamism of the surrounding wall. Another sculptural example (see Fig.3g), the sixth-century stele from Parel, near Bombay, shows a multiple emanation of figures.[7]

h) Gyration. This principle does not directly convey emergence and expansion, but may accompany them. Stellate shrines (on a star-shaped plan) give the impression that they turn at the same time as they centrifugally unfurl. The eye is drawn around the circumference from one radial aedicule-chain to another.

The working together of these principles will now be illustrated, in both Nāgara and Drāviḍa examples.

In the movement patterns of Nāgara temples an essential part is played by the *gavākṣa*. As well as representing a dormer window projecting from thatched eaves, the motif also stems from the gables on early rock-cut *caitya* hall facades, and implies the presence of a thatched barrel-roof behind, embedded. Through embeddedness and projection the *gavākṣa* has an inherent directional thrust. This is augmented by other devices, particularly the idea of splitting. A simple configuration (Fig.4c, right) is a *gavākṣa* flanked by two half-*gavākṣas*, giving the impression that one emergent *gavākṣa* has split, and as the two halves move apart another *gavākṣa* is appearing from within. Fig.4e illustrates the dynamics of this kind of pattern bursting through one pair of mouldings in the central spine of the *śikhara* at the Galaganatha, Pattadakal (early eighth century). Cascading down the *śikhara*, the *gavākṣas* unfurl like a string of *mantras*. Their window

a. Caitya hall cross-section

b. Aedicule in a Gandharan relief C2 A.D.

c. Simple composite gavākṣa-configurations

d.

e.

f.

f,g: Telikā Mandir Gwalior

d,e: Galaganātha, Paṭṭadakal Pediment of niche (gavākṣa-aedicule) and dynamics of central lāta (spine) of śikhara

g.

Fig. 4 Gavaksa Patterns

character is evident in the way in which they reveal an inner space, consisting of receding vistas through planes of a schematic colonnade.

Another pattern, with roots at least as early as second-century Gandhara (Fig.4b), consists of a complete *gavākṣa* resting on two half-*gavākṣas*. As a pillar is shown, in early examples, within each half-*gavākṣa*, it is not difficult to see that the form originated as a schematic rendering of the cross-section, or front elevation, of a *caitya* hall. But the pattern is soon exploited for the expression of movement, through the notion that the top *gavākṣa* has emerged first, and the second has come through and split. This idea is reinforced when further, enshrined motifs show a continuation of the process (Fig.4d). The dynamics of the Valabhī mode of temple, such as the Telika Mandir, Gwalior (circa 700-750) can be understood through this concept, used in conjunction with multiple enshrinement, and staggering of the wall; a sense of upward expansion is also present, through 'expanding repetition' (Figs.4f-g, 5).

Simple *gavākṣa* configurations such as the two kinds discussed so far are built up into complex expanding constellations, in which the principle of 'progressive multiplication' is used to show the division of one into many. At a certain stage the idea of overlap is introduced—of some *gavākṣas* shown in front of others—enhancing the sense of sequence (as in Fig.12).

It is in temples belonging to the Śekharī mode that the expression of movement in Nāgara architecture is greatest.[8] By the time this mode is formed, *gavākṣa* patterns have been knitted into a lacy net (*jāla*), veiling the *śikhara* eaves-mouldings, while other such patterns, at a larger scale, are still used to create telescopically unfolding pediments. But in the overall dynamism these devices merely serve to reinforce the more powerful interplay of *śikhara* forms. On the principle of projection of embedded forms, four minor *śikhara* (and by implication, four embedded Latina *prāsādas*) are shown half-emerged from the four faces of the central *śikhara*. Along the cardinal axes of the *mūlaprāsāda* may emerge further, lesser *śikhara* forms, in diminishing sequences. These sequences continue to evolve through *gavākṣa* pediments or giant *gavākṣas* crowning the central projection of the wall below, and in through minor aedicules in the wall, or even in the plinth. Where 'quarter-*śikharas*' (three-quarters-embedded *śikharas*) are shown at the sides of the 'half-*śikhara*', as in the Kandariya Mahadeva, Khajuraho (Figs.6, 7), the main pattern of the whole, of four emerging from one, is reflected in the parts. The expanding universe revealed by

Fig. 5 Telika Mandir, Gwalior

the principal *śikhara* forms, dissolving in the very process of manifestation, is explained by Fig.8.

This orthogonal expansion is accompanied by an all-round growth through a 'progressive multiplication' of *kūṭastambhas* pouring down the corners (Fig.3e). Figure 7 shows the extent to which, in the Kandariya Mahadeva, the *kūṭastambhas* and other forms interpenetrate.

Simultaneous with the downward and outward forces, the Śekhari form of organisation creates a powerful upward surge. As the growing forms radiate and descend, the whole temple, like an expanding *liṅga*,

Fig. 6 Kandariya Mahadeva, Khajuraho

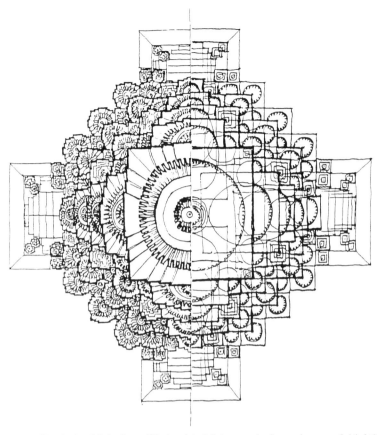

Fig. 7 Kandariya Mahadeva, Khajuraho; Mulaprasada from above and (right)
showing interpenetration

swells up and smoothly rockets towards the heavens. This effect is
brought about through the upward drift of 'expanding repetition'
among the *śikhara* forms (Fig.3f).

    While embeddedness is fundamental to the Drāviḍa architecture of
Tamilnad, and while this architecture evolves devices such as the split
pilaster (Fig.3c) which explicitly convey emergence, dynamic forces
are never as pervasive in the temples of that region as they are
elsewhere. The Karṇāṭa Drāviḍa, on the other hand, reaches extreme
dynamism in its later Calukya development, sometimes identified as
'Vesara' (a well-known example is the Mahadeva, Ittagi, Fig.9). Here
aedicular articulation has been extended through all *talas* (storeys) of
the pyramidal structure (the top *tala*, together with the 'dome', having
previously been treated as a unitary *alpa vimāna*). The aedicular
components of each *tala* are identical in number and type, ensuring a
radial continuity which allows 'expanding repetition' through
descending bands. Through a staggered plan, stepping out progressively

Fig. 8 Dynamics of the Kandariya Mahadeva, Khajuraho

Fig. 9 Mahadevi, Ittagi (photo courtesy of Gerard Foekema)

from corners to centre, each face grows with an axial bulge. The degree
of interpenetration among the de-telescoping *talas* is shown in Fig.10.

Staggering in the whole is accompanied by staggering in the parts,
which mirror the sequential swell and centrifugal dissolution of the
whole. This is most dramatic in the double-staggered central *śālā*-
aedicules (Fig.11c). In these a *pañjara*-aedicule (see Fig.2a) puts forth
one *śālā*-aedicule to either side, and from each of these a further
embedded *śālā*-aedicule emerges laterally. The forward and sideways
motion is emphasised by the pictorially represented outpourings of each
gable-end *nāsī* (horseshoe arch) from a lion-face finial, whose snail-
like buttress-body rides along on the *śālā* roof-ridge.

Fig. 10 Interpenetration in a late Karnata Dravida Vimana

a. Śālās (single-staggered) with single nāsi (left) and double nāsi (right).

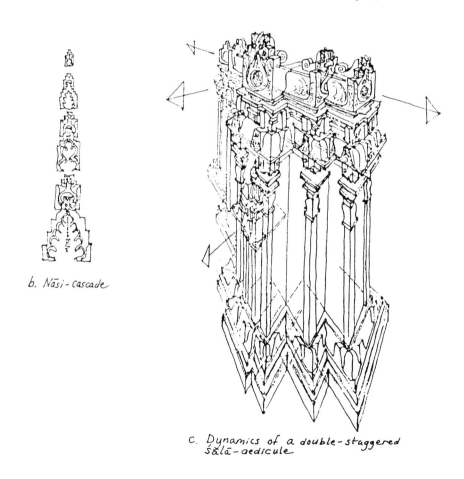

b. Nāsi-cascade

c. Dynamics of a double-staggered śālā-aedicule

Fig. 11 Late Karnata Dravida ('Vesara') Vimana: Dynamics of Central Projection

An invention which enhances the sense of emanation in the *nāsī* is the 'double *nāsī*' (Fig.11a), whereby, in the central *pañjara* of a *śālā*, the original *nāsī* gives birth to another *nāsī*, or to a *toraṇa* (arch), with its own monster-finial, issuing through the lower mouldings of the parapet. Where this device is used, the cardinal *nāsīs* of the dome originate central cascades of vegetal arch-forms, flowing down each face of the *vimāna* (Fig.11b). Minor *nāsī*-cascades echo elsewhere.

In the first *tala* of a late Karṇāṭa Drāviḍa ('Vesara') *vimāna*, wall-shrines (aedicular niches) emerge from the primary aedicules, sometimes exuding further, lesser wall-shrines. The sense of emergence is made more forceful through a bursting of boundaries (Fig.3d) by which wall-shrines break out across the framing pilasters and beyond. This happens most where expression most demands it, at the forwardmost bulge of the expanding wall, where giant wall-shrines may even pierce the upper limit of the wall-zone and enter the parapet.

Evolution

The process represented in the formal structure of these temples, a growth from an invisible point towards an ultimate dissolution which can only vaguely be sensed, has a striking parallel in the pattern of development of the temple forms during the course of their respective traditions. This pattern too, if a broad enough perspective is taken, can be seen to burgeon out from the seed of simple unity towards the ocean of complex unity (though neither end of such a flow is realisable in a human artifact).

This simultaneous differentiation and fusion, creation and dissolution, emergence and merging takes place in architectural form through the operation of certain specific tendencies which may be traced through the course of a tradition. Such trends are not necessarily manifested continuously nor at an even rate. The degree of 'development' is always partly a function of the scale and importance of a work, and at any time the range of possibilities includes various levels of complexity. But these observations do not obscure the overall evolutionary picture, if a tradition is considered as a whole.

The principal evolutionary tendencies are as follows:

a)   Aedicularity. The principle of articulating the temple exterior as a matrix of interconnected shrine-images takes increasing hold, progressively extended down a hierarchy from primary components to minor niches.

b)   Aedicular density. Shrine images are moved closer together, and secondary and tertiary aedicules increasingly embedded within the primary ones. Eventually an overflowing compression and fullness is arrived at through multiple interpenetration.

c) Proliferation and fragmentation. Aedicular density presupposes a proliferation of aedicular forms. This is accompanied by a proliferation of exterior mouldings within these. Fragmentation is an inevitable outcome of proliferation, since the multiplication of parts amounts to a breaking-up of the whole. Surfaces are increasingly fractured by staggering (see (f) below) and individual elements come to be represented as having split apart (Fig.3c).

d) Central emphasis. The cardinal axes of the temple as a whole become increasingly dominant, and a similar process occurs within the aedicular components, at the various levels of order.

e) Movement. There is an increasing use of the various formal patterns which I have interpreted as means of conveying a sense of emergence and expansion.

f) Staggering. Forms become progressively more staggered, from the plan as a whole, through the aedicular components and pillars, to the mouldings of pilasters.

g) Continuity/alignment. The horizontal continuity inherent in a wall built up of superimposed mouldings becomes emphasised by the flattening out of profiles, the atrophy of wide recesses, the division of certain mouldings by a horizontal fillet, and sometimes the division of the wall zone. Vertical continuity becomes established and emphasised through the alignment of certain elements one above the other.[9]

h) Abstraction. Architectural imagery, particularly in the shapes of mouldings, develops away from the depiction of timber and thatch construction, transformed by formal, rather than representational needs.

i) Assimilation. Elements or details at first only vaguely related in shape become explicitly so.

To give the bare outline of the evolutionary phenomenon, Fig.12 gives an 'idealised' picture of the evolution respectively of the Karṇāṭa Draviḍa, of gavākṣa patterns, and of the Śekharī mode of Nāgara. The single gavākṣa is progressively multiplied, fragmented, overlapped and woven into an intricate mesh, in which the individual motif is all but lost. At the base of the unitary Latina mūlaprāsāda (right) appear miniature śikharas in relief, which round out into half-embedded śikharas and, with the wall-segments below, into kūṭastambhas. Further proliferation, further fragmentation of the whole, brings forth further śikhara forms and kūṭastambhas, more and more densely interpenetrating, the pregnant wall bulging ever forward, until corners are lost in the stepped diamond plan. In the Karṇāṭa Draviḍa tradition

Karṇāṭa Drāviḍa   Nāgara (gavākṣas)   Nāgara (Śekhari)

Fig. 12 Evolution in Temple Types

(Fig.12, left), from the unitary *alpa vimāna* springs the tiered pyramid, from which emerge, progressively, the cloistered shrine images, and lesser versions from these. Parts lose hold in the central surge, as surfaces crumple, and one by one appear the increasingly staggered, overlapped aediculae. Eventually, as diagonal forces begin to push out, and still the centre swells, the bubble bursts, and everything settles into the centreless, cornerless, all-identical, descending spiral fusion of the uniform stallate *vimāna* form (see Fig.3h).

It is a way of growth that is inherent in the shape of these traditions, a predisposition, not predestination. Thus, it is possible to imagine that, in different historical circumstances, a 'fused' Karṇāṭa Draviḍa *vimāna* form, once again unitary, might have become the starting point for a new cycle. Indeed, in northern temple architecture two broad cycles are apparent, although the earlier one is no longer traceable through every stage. The temples of Dakshina Kosala are, from as early as the end of the sixth century, fully multi-aedicular, yet clearly the predecessors of the unitary Latina *prāsāda*, which in turn would become the matrix and the principal aedicular component of further composition forms.

Through this way of growth, with its propensity to be cyclical, aspects of the architectural vocabulary may undergo a cycle that is not in step with the broader cycle through which the overall form is passing. In this way the *gavākṣa* reaches the proliferated, fragmented, overlapped, abstracted fusion of the *jāla* net well before the comparable transformation of the whole Nāgara *prāsāda*.

Two notable aspects of the single evolutionary scheme can be discerned. These are complementary, and neither is fully understandable without the other, but it is useful to distinguish between the two. The first, which may be termed 'illusionistic', is an aspect of the evolution which can be visualised as a process similar to the patterns of movement represented in *vimānas*. In this respect, the parallel between the patterns of change in the tradition and the single monument are direct and concrete. The 'illusionistic' operation of the evolutionary tendencies is accompanied by a process which may be called 'conceptual', concerning an observer's perception and conception of the architectural parts in relation to each other and to the whole. During the course of the tradition the parts of a *vimāna* composition, in the very process of their articulation, lose stability and individuality under the sway of the whole. This 'conceptual' process of the coming into being and simultaneous subsumation of architectural components is, from the point of view of the whole composition, a break-down of the simple whole of the earliest temples, and at the same time a fusion into a complex whole. The resulting complexity is such that the attention tends to rest only fleetingly on individual elements or configurations, while to contemplate the totality is to sense a fertile, oceanic, overflowing continuum, ever on the point of bursting into differentiation (for example, Fig.9). It should again be stressed that the 'conceptual' and 'illusionistic' do not operate in isolation, so that however self-contained may seem the system of interrelationships within the temple exterior, dynamic outflow ensures that ultimate completion is conceived as something infinitely beyond.

The palpable inclination of the temple architects to portray a particular kind of movement partly explains the character of the evolution, particularly of its 'illusionistic' aspect. The direct parallel which the 'illusionistic' aspect of the evolution shows with the dynamic structure of a *vimāna* or *mūlaprāsāda* is largely explicable in terms of this propensity, whether or not it is a conscious intention or aim. If, hypothetically, an artistic tradition develops in pursuit of, say, refinement, smoothness or complexity, a single work will not encapsulate a process of refining, smoothing or complicating, but simply exemplify a particular stage in the process. In such cases an impression of evolution in an individual work will arise only through the recollection of previous norms. But where a desired effect is the impression of development through time, architectural form embodies a process of evolution which has taken place in the course of the tradition.

Thus the processes of proliferation, conveyed by 'progressive multiplication', and of fragmentation, conveyed by 'splitting', are both developments which take place as the tradition advances. Every movement pattern rendered in stone portrays a sequence of two or more stages, and may imply or even incorporate stages which have actually occurred in earlier monuments. Staggering records the process of staggering: a staggered wall implies a formerly flat wall, and the double-staggered *śālā*-aedicule contains an earlier, single-staggered version. Prior containment is implicit where a wall-shrine bursts from its frame, and a double *nāsī* includes the original single *nāsī*.

Moreover, in the development of the form of the *vimāna* as a whole can be traced cumulative sequences in which successive stages, expanding downwards, incorporate the preceding version. A sequence of this kind is shown in Fig.10 (left). One *vimāna* form becomes the 'upper temple' of a more advanced form, which in turn becomes the 'upper temple' for yet another form. A similar sequence is shown in the development of the Śekhari *mūlaprāsāda*, and in a comparable kind of progressive incorporation among *gavākṣa* patterns, whereby earlier, simpler configurations are used to compose more complex ones, which in turn are combined into others yet more complex.

The 'conceptual' aspect of the evolution might be explained by the notion that, consciously or unconsciously, the artists strove for the trance-like effect of a unified field, brimming with multiple entities and configurations, which become centres of attention only momentarily, before being caught in an expanding web of relationships, built up in stages towards an elusive totality.

Meaning

Discussion of meaning in architecture usually focuses on secondary, extrinsic ideas attached to forms by association, ignoring the symbolism which is truly inherent by virtue of the direct analogy or congruence between ideas and formal pattern. In the case of Indian temples there is this kind of correspondence, as I have already suggested, between the compositional structure and an Indian perception of manifestation, of the coming into concrete form of the divinity and, on a cosmic level, of the transmutation of the eternal and infinite into the shifting multiplicity of existence, and the reabsorption of all things into the limitless unity from which they have come.

It has already been shown that this symbolism of formal structure is not entirely abstract, nor divorced from representational imagery. Formal structure would not have become what it is, nor developed the way it has, were it not for what it directly depicts. A third mechanism of meaning is association. Within a culture, certain ideas may become associated with certain forms or motifs, not as mere unambiguous signs, but as symbols with multiple metaphoric overtones, vague and productive. A network of associations, built up as much in the realms of myth and poetry as of architecture and sculpture, binds particular forms one to another. In Indian temples, as in much sacred architecture, motifs or elements (such as the lotus and the horseshoe arch) which by their nature lend themselves as symbols of the Centre, seem especially susceptible to incorporation into such a web of significance. But however 'natural' it may seem at times, it is difficult to see how associational meaning can be intrinsic in the same way as the other two kinds, or knowable so directly from buildings themselves. Yet in the original cultural context of the temples, these three kinds of symbolism, 'formal', representational and associational, must have worked together, inseparably, reinforcing one another.

The school of thought that owes much in this century to A.K. Coomaraswamy, adhering to the 'perennial philosophy' found in Platonism and the Vedanta, is concerned (on the basis of multiple levels of existence) with symbols as reflections of divine archetypes, and therefore divinely given, 'adequate' and intrinsic. A 'real art' is one of 'symbolic and significant representation; a representation of things that cannot be seen except by the intellect'.[10] The problem with this insight, in interpreting works of art, is that it tends to do away with the need to show *how* symbolism works, whereas here we have been discussing meaning that is intrinsic by virtue of the actual properties of form. With this proviso, the conclusion of this paper will be close to Coomaraswamy's view.

Method

What is the evidence that this way of seeing a particular kind of architecture comes close to the principles underlying its conception? The first and most important test of an architectural interpretation is that it should be possible for it to be clearly visualised, and for the visualisation, through words or images, to be communicated. A given architecture asks to be seen in a particular way (or a set of complementary ways which allow productive ambiguity). The way of seeing Indian temples which we have been exploring allows the absolutely distinct seeing in the mind's eye of the totality of an architectural conception. Such instant visualisation, and hence succinct description of overall, composition, is made possible by the 'aedicular' way of seeing that I have put forward.

The dynamic patterns that follow on from aedicularity are also fully visualisable, although communication of the vision in its entirety can be more difficult in this case; perhaps computer animation might become a tool for 'proving' that certain ways of seeing are possible, while others are not. (Sculptural representations, incidentally, provide direct visual evidence for the idea of downward and outward flow: monster jaws disgorging foliant arches, finial faces, pilasters and *gavākṣas* split down the middle.) Visualisation is equally a test for the validity of the closely analogous *evolutionary* pattern that I have described. The same blossoming out that is captured in a single shrine can be experienced when the tradition, devoured and digested, is run through the mind like the speeded-up film of an opening flower.

Another test of an interpretation or way of seeing (and a corresponding method of analysis) is its explanatory power, dependent upon the consistency and pervasiveness of the patterns which it reveals, the order and sense which it brings to complex architectural forms, and its capacity to explain both the variations and permutations among monuments of a given time, and the way in which architecture develops through time. Thus, for example, Drāviḍa temples can be seen in terms only of horizontal divisions—base, wall, parapet—ignoring the vertical connections which create the aedicules; but such a limited way of looking does not allow the succinct description of whole compositions that the aedicular interpretation allows, nor an awareness of represented movement, which in turn explains, to some extent, the mode of development.

In relation to a search for evidence, this 'methodology of seeing' is not a visionary substitute for systematic formal analysis, but a prerequisite for it, if the analysis is not to become senseless cataloguing. A way of seeing, grasped intuitively, may be substantiated by minute observation. So, for example, each general 'evolutionary tendency' in a tradition can be illustrated by detailed tabulation of developments among particular examples.[11] Of course it is important not to create a circular argument, by taking an apparent pattern of development as evidence of chronological sequence. Ancient Indian works of art and buildings are notoriously difficult to date, in the absence of historical chronicles. But, in a wide perspective, over a long time-span, it is sufficient for there to be a few securely dated works to confirm the general picture.

A way of seeing architecture finds further resonance, if not 'proof', by reference to other aspects of culture. For example, a dynamic conception of the universe can be pointed out with reference to Sanskrit etymology: *ṛta* (order) is from the root *ṛ*, to go, *jagat* (universe) from the root *gam*, to go or move, *nabh* (navel) from the root *nabh*, to expand, and so on. Mythology can be called upon: a vision of emerging and expanding form is depicted in the *liṅgodbhava* myth (see 'Pictorial Representation' above).

But these are parallels, and do not validate the way of seeing to the same extent as the deep correspondence between the dynamic architectural structure of sequential emergence, growth and subsequent reabsorption, and perennial Indian ideas about the nature of manifestation, about the relationship of god to the world. This interpretation, if metaphysical, is not just 'read into' the forms, but firmly tied to the physical actuality of the architecture. The forms make these ideas concrete, just as the ideas make sense of the formal structure. Nevertheless, it can be argued by a committed Positivist that the logic here is one of correspondences rather than of causality, that there can be no 'proof' of a connection.[12] Why not, then, put meaning aside for the sake of scholarly argument, and leave it, as for a while I thought I should, merely as a suggestive undercurrent to the more irrefutable discussion of form? I shall return to this question shortly.

Meanwhile, for those for whom the forms themselves are insufficient evidence that they embody manifestation, taking place through successive emanations, textual and iconographic evidence is at hand. The eleventh-century western Indian Vāstuśāstra of Viśvakarma, in a chapter on the rite of 'placement' of deities in the parts of a temple, including the various mouldings, says, 'Let the five divinities— Brahmā, Viṣṇu, Rudra, Īśvara [Maheśa] and Sadāśiva—live in [each] urah-śṛṅga on each bhadra offset'.[13] Urah-śṛṅgas or 'chest-sproutings' are the main, aedicular components of the Śekhari mode of Nāgara temple (see Fig.2b). The sequential emergence of these forms was clearly recognised in the Vāstuśāstra, since the series of divinities invoked is (from last to lowest emanation to first and highest) the emanatory hierarchy of the Śaiva Siddhānta system.[14]

That the same way of representing emanation is still understood is clear from a modern print which I saw recently. It shows a giant Viṣṇu, with Sai Baba, the nineteenth-century Maharashtrian holy man, emerging like an urah-śṛṅga from Viṣṇu's chest, while below and directly in front of this Sai Baba appears Sai Baba the present-day guru. The message is not difficult to read: Sai Baba was an avatar of Viṣṇu, and the new Sai Baba is an avatar of the old one.

In her studies of Śaiva iconography, Doris Srinivasan explains the vedic and upanishadic ideas of how, in a threefold sequence, 'the all-pervasive, transcendental Supreme is connected to the material form of god',[15] and shows that the medieval Śaiva āgamas describe just such a sequence in their doctrine of the unfolding of the triple Śiva reality from transcendency to materiality. Para Śiva, formless and undifferentiated (niṣkala) gives rise to Sadāśva between formlessness and full manifestation (sakala-niṣkala), who emanates Maheśa, with form (sakala). Para Śiva is shown to have been represented by the plain liṅga, Sadāśiva by the mukha-liṅga—a liṅga with faces emerging on the cardinal axes (with a fifth, not usually represented, on top, looking up), and Maheśa by full anthropomorphic forms of Śiva. A complex sixth-century liṅga from Kalyanpur (Rajasthan) combines all three in a temple-like composition,[16] with the degree of exposure denoting the degree of manifestation. On the cardinal axes of the central plain liṅga (Para Śiva) emerge the heads and shoulders of Sadyojāta, Aghora, Tatpuruṣa and Vāmadeva, aspects of Sadāśiva. From the chests of these, at the base of the composition, emerge small, fully-exposed images of four manifestations of Maheśa: Śiva, Viṣṇu, Sūrya and Brahmā.

'The unfolding proceeds downward, as in a birth', writes Doris Srinivasan, deducing by skilful correlation of texts and iconography what can already be seen in the forms. Another iconographic scheme which she analyses is that of the central west spine (latā) in the śikhasa of the Parasurameshvara at Bhuvaneshvara (Orissa).[17] The images inside the gavākṣas (horseshoe arches), as if descending from the finial (formless Para Śiva of the śikhara, are: a lotus—Sadāśiva with one head and shoulders—as a mukha-liṅga—Lakulīśa (a manifestation of Maheśa)—Nateśa (Maheśa as cosmic creator)—and Rāvaṇā-nugrahamūrti (a minor manifestation of Maheśa). This iconographic sequence parallels the unfurling of the gavākṣa-chain, which is similar to the pattern which I explain in Fig.4e.

To return to the question of meaning, it would be wrong to conclude from all of this that temple forms (as opposed, possibly, to sculptural iconography) could somehow be a deliberate translation of a precise doctrine, or that particular philosophical or mythological systems could be literally expounded in stone. Temple architecture (independently of carved images or invocatory rites) will not portray a particular theological hierarchy, but embody a more underlying vision. It will not in itself show who emanates whom, but will allow sequences of divinities to be read into or carved onto it, because it shares with those sequences the same intuition of a serially emanating cosmos. The sacred architecture of the temples is the presentation of an experience, of an intuition of higher truth, which (in the Vedantic view) is beyond space and time.

Ultimately, then, certainly in a sacred architecture, form cannot be separated from meaning. While it may be shown beyond doubt, concentrating on form alone, that architectural composition is as it is and develops as it does, the question of why this is so cannot be answered fully if meaning is ignored. We have found partial answers in the apparent intentions, conscious or unconscious, of the temple builders, to express ('illusionistically') emergence, expansion and simultaneous dissolution, and to convey ('conceptually') the sense of an undifferentiated yet super-fertile, overflowing continuum. But the question of why anyone should have such intentions points ultimately to the transcendent meaning which these architectural forms and these verbal formulations both embody.

A pyramid of gods' names or of chiselled stones gives local habitation to a sense of emanatory hierarchy, itself a formulation of something beyond all grasp; it is only by making tangible, whether in concepts, sounds or masonry, an intuition of what is beyond form, that meaning can take shape, and ideas and powers be thought about and experienced. The paradigms of Indian architecture are in Heaven.

---

[1] Quoted in Alain Daniélou, *The Gods of India* (New York, 1985), p.6, fn.3.

[2] In particular, the temples built from around the sixth century to around the fourteenth, mainly Hindu and Jain. I have developed the main ideas of this paper in Adam Hardy, *Indian Temple Architecture: form and transformation* (New Delhi, 1994), which is a revised version of 'The Karṇāṭa Drāviḍa Tradition: development of Indian temple architecture in Karnataka, 7th-13th centuries', PhD thesis, CNAA, 1991.

[3] Geoffrey Scott, *The Architecture of Humanism* (London, 1914) was a forerunner of this scepticism. See also, for example, David Watkin, *Morality and Architecture* (Oxford, 1977); Sir Ernst Gombrich, for example, in *The Sense of Order* (Oxford, 1979). The writings of the philosopher Karl Popper have formed a basis for a critique of evolutionism by Gombrich and others; see Popper's *The Poverty of Historicism* (London, 1961).

[4] 'A symbolic interpretation of a work of art can be compared to the waves generated by a stone thrown into the water. Following the widening circles on the surface, one soon loses sight of the stone, which meanwhile is sinking beyond recovery. Symbolic interpretations are surface interpretations, while formal ones are interpretations in depth. In short, symbolic interpretations are after effects of a work of art. To postulate, in addition to the aesthetic monism of form-meaning, an aesthetic dualism of form-meaning plus symbolism, is to obscure the primarily formal nature of the visual arts'; P. Fingeston, *The Eclipse of Symbolism* (South Carolina, 1970), p.102.

[5] The idea of the temple as a symbol of manifestation was put forward by Stella Kramrisch: 'The temple is the concrete shape (mūrti) of the Essence; as such it is the residence and vesture of God. The masonry is the sheath (kośa) and body. The temple is the monument of manifestation. The devotee who comes to the temple, to look at it, does so as a seer, not as a spectator'; Kramrisch, *The Hindu Temple* (Calcutta, 1946), p.165). Kramrisch also sees movement in the temple structure, though without tying this insight to concrete characteristics of architectural forms: 'Its [the temple's] mantle carries, imaged in its varied texture, in all directions, all the forms and principles of manifestation towards the Highest Point above the body of the temple' (1946, p.361). But it is downwards as well as outwards that will be seen to be the predominant directions of the unfolding represented by the architectural forms, even if the summit is sensed as receding upwards as the whole shrine expands. It is thus outwards and downwards which call to be experienced as the directions of manifestation, with inwards and upwards as the directions of the devotee's aspiration towards union. Significantly, in Sanskrit '*Agre*, "at the beginning", is literally "the top-point"'; Betty Heimann, *Facets of Indian Thought* (London, 1964), p.121.

[6] The term 'aedicule' is normally used for the architectural framework around niches or windows in European Classical architecture, representing a miniature building, usually with two pilasters supporting an entablature

(including pediment). The meaning of the term has been extended by John Summerson, 'Heavenly Mansions: an interpretation of Gothic', *Heavenly Mansions and other essays on architecture* (London, 1949), to imply any miniature representation of a building used as an element of architectural composition. Summerson quotes James Fergusson (1876, p.285), who wrote that 'everywhere...in India, architectural decoration is made up of small models of large buildings'. In spite of this early observation by Fergusson the aedicular character of Indian temple architecture has not been sufficiently emphasised by writers on the subject. Individual motifs have of course been recognised as miniature shrines, but it has not been clearly stated, and perhaps not clearly seen, that, in its developed forms, this architecture depends for its visual structure, its expression and meanings, on the combination and interrelation of images of shrines.

[7] 'The phenomenon of the expanding form' in Indian art is interpreted, using sculptural examples, as an expression of a dynamic view of the universe by Heinrich Zimmer in Joseph Campbell (ed.), *Myths and Symbols in Indian Art and Civilization* (New York, 1946), pp.130-6. Both these examples of 'pictorial representation' are cited by Zimmer (Figs.30, 32). Referring to the liṅgodbhava image in the Musée Guimet, Paris, Zimmer writes (p.130): "The solid, static mass of stone, by a subtle artifice of the craftsman, has been converted into a dynamorphic event. In this respect, this piece of sculpture is more like a motion picture than a painting. The notion that there is nothing static, nothing abiding, but only the flow of a relentless process, with everything originating, growing, decaying, vanishing—this wholly dynamic view of life, of the individual and of the universe, is one of the fundamental conceptions (as we have seen) of later Hinduism'.

[8] The Śekhari is one of the two composite modes of Nāgara that emerged around the tenth century. The other is the Bhūmija, of central and western India, in which the segments of the Patina, with the exception of the cardinal projections, are replaced by radiating bands of *kūṭastambhas*.

[9] In Karṇāṭa Draviḍa temples, radial continuity, inherent in Nāgara, with inclined bands of elements descending from the *vimāna* summit, is the rule by the end of the Early Calukya period, and later becomes more emphatic. This is a prerequisite of expanding repetition among primary aedicules, and of central emphasis.

[10] A.K. Coomaraswamy, 'Why exhibit works of art?', in *Christian and Oriental Philosophy of Art* (New York, 1956), p.11. By 'intellect', Commaraswamy means the supra-individual *buddhi*.

[11] See Table 1 in Hardy, 'Indian Temple Architecture'.

[12] For a discussion of symbolism and the 'logic of correspondencies' from a phenomenological perspective, see Jacques Macquett, *The Aesthetic Experience* (Yale, 1986).

[13] M.A. Dhaky, 'Prāsāda as Cosmos', the *Adiyar Library Bulletin*, XXXV, 3-4 (Madras, 1971), p.216.

[14] In 'The Structure of Time in the Kandariyā Mahādeva Temple of Khajuraho' (paper given at seminar on time, at IGNCA, Delhi 1990), Devangana Desai has correlated this Śaiva Siddhānta system with the iconography of that temple, and pointed out the passage about *uraḥ-śṛṅgas* discovered by Dhaky in the Vāstuśāstra of Viśvakarma.

[15] Doris Meth Srinivasan, 'From transcendency to materiality: Para Śiva Sadāśiva, and Maheśa in Indian art', in *Artibus Asiae* L, 1/2 (1990), p.108. See also 'Śaiva temple forms: loci of God's unfolding body', in M. Yaldiz and W. Labo (eds.), *Investigating Indian Art* (Berlin, 1987).

[16] Ibid., pp.337-40.

[17] Srinivasan, 'From transcendency to materiality', pp.129-31.

Chapter Six

GODS, PATRONS AND IMAGES:
STONE SCULPTURE AT VIJAYANAGARA

Anna L. Dallapiccola

The great city of Bizenegalia is situated near very steep mountains. The circumference of the city is 60 miles; its walls are carried up to the mountains and enclose the valleys at their foot.... In this city there are estimated to be ninety thousand men fit to bear arms.... [1]

The visitor whose impressions are described in the above quotation was the Venetian merchant Nicolò de Conti who started his journey to the East in about 1419. The first Indian town he visited was Khambayat (Cambay) and he continued his journey travelling southwards along the western coast. Disembarking either in Pacamuria (Barakuru) or Helly (this might just be the Kanarese word for village, *halli*) he started for an inland tour to see the splendours of the kingdom of 'Bizenegalia' (such is the fifteenth-century Italian deformation of the name Vijayanagara). He was the first European visitor, whose account has come down to us, to visit the capital. He noted, amongst other things, the chariot festival, the Divali and the Mahanavami celebrations.

Shortly afterwards, Abdur Razzaq, the emissary sent to India by the ruler of Herat, arrived at Vijayanagara during the reign of Devaraya II (1424-1446). In the preface to his chronicle he declared that the inhabitants of Vijayanagara 'have no equals in the world'. He was so impressed that, in an enthusiastic passage he says:

> The pupil of the eye has never seen a place like it, and the ear of Intelligence has never been informed that there existed anything to equal it in the world.[2]

Only after passing through seven concentric fortifications, Abdur Razzaq finally arrived at the innermost palace of the king where he observed an audience hall, a hall of justice, the hall of the chief minister, and the mint. He also noted the elephant stables, each animal having its own compartment, and, of course, the bazaars skirting long colonnaded streets.

Before considering the chronicles of the Portuguese visitors, another Italian visitor should be mentioned, Ludovico de Varthema from Bologna, who left Europe in 1502 and via Cairo, Damascus, Aden and

Persia reached Gujarat and the southern coast of India. He landed at Mangalur, and later visited Vijayanagara which he described as a great city 'very large and strong walled. It is situated on the side of a mountain…. It has a triple circlet of walls'. It was a very wealthy and well-supplied city, situated on a beautiful site and enjoying an excellent climate.[3]

The first known Portuguese who entered Vijayanagara must have been Duarte Barbosa. This visit is thought to have taken place in the year 1508/9. In his *Livro em qua da relacao de que viu o ouviu no Oriente*, he mentions the sea trade on the western coast of the Vijayanagara empire. Among other visitors in the opening years of the sixteenth century were the famous Domingo Paes and Fernao Nunes, who chronicled their visits in the *Chronicas do reis de Bisnaga*. Paes' account is earlier (pre-1535) and gives detailed information about the site and its buildings. Paes was overawed by the size and wealth of the city:

> The size of the city I do not write here, because it cannot all be seen from any one spot, but I climbed a hill whence I could see a great part of it; I could not see it all because it lies between several ranges of hills. What I saw from thence seemed to me as large as Rome, and very beautiful to the sight; there are many groves of trees within it, in the gardens of the houses, and many conduits of water which flow into the midst of it, and in palaces there are lakes; the king has close to his palace a palm grove and other rich fruit-bearing trees….
>
> This is the best provided city in the world, and is stocked with provisions such as rice, wheat and grains, Indian-corn and a certain amount of barley and beans, moong, pulses…. The streets and markets are full of laden oxen without count so that you cannot get along for them, and in many streets you come upon so many of them that you have to wait for them to pass, or else have to go by another way.[4]

From the wealth of material contained in this account, I would like to extract parts of Paes' report of Vijayanagara buildings, especially of the temples:

> Outside the city walls on the north there are three very beautiful pagodas, one of which is called Vitella, and it stands over against this city of Nagundym, and the other is called Aoperadianar, and this is the one which they hold most in veneration, and to which they make great pilgrimages.[5]

Sculptures are continually mentioned: those decorating the gopura of the Virupaksha (Aoperadianar) temple; others on the parapets of the private houses in the main streets—'You will see rows of houses with many figures and decorations pleasing to look at'[6]—and, finally, the woodcarvings decorating the various temple chariots of the town.

This was a city in a class of its own; it was famous in the traders' world, so much so that Vijayanagara is mentioned in the *Arabian Nights* as the place where the world-renowned 'flying carpet' was bought by Prince Ali.[7] The brutal sack of the town by the troops of the confederated Deccani Sultans and the vandalisation of most of its monuments in 1565, however, put an end to this splendour.

Despite visitors' unanimously enthusiastic reports, and their commendation of the citizens' aesthetic sensitivity, expressed in buildings, sculptures and in paintings—especially wall paintings and paintings on cloth—Vijayanagara art in general, and sculpture in particular, have not been a popular subject with art historians. Except for some brief notices in general works dealing with Indian art, few scholars have shown a consistent interest in the subject. There are several reasons for this. Foremost are the rather unflattering opinions on the aesthetic qualities of the 'Vijayanagara style' given by scholars such as A. Rea: 'As regards the style of Vijayanagara there is hardly anything to single it out',[8] and Vincent A. Smith, who dubbed it in his *History of Fine Art*, published in 1911, as 'local' and 'semi-barbaric'.[9] Almost a century has passed since these statements were made, but there is still a certain reluctance in the scholarly world to recognise the artistic merits of these works.

Furthermore, Vijayanagara art has been neglected because it falls into a 'late period' in the history of Indian art and hence is implicitly considered 'decadent' according to the Western perception of a linear stylistic development in a given time-frame. For example, Hermann Goetz, who was among those who wrote repeatedly on Vijayanagara, referred in his lectures to the Vijayanagara style as either 'decadent' or 'folkish', depending on whether he was describing some of the late temples or the sculptures on the Mahanavami platform. The underlying assumption was that the period was not worthy of serious study.

The third reason is that Vijayanagara and its successor, Nayaka art, were not within the sphere of interest of those studying Buddhist and Hindu art, since historically speaking, the Vijayanagara era coincides with what is considered to be the 'Islamic period', while those concerned with Islamic art in the northern part of India and the Deccan considered the contemporary artistic activity at the Hindu courts in southern India to be outside their concern.

The focus of art-historical enquiry, as far as the Vijayanagara period is concerned, has concentrated on temple architecture with sculpture merely noted as an integral part of architecture. As Percy Brown states:

> Much of the intricacy and beauty of the Vijayanagar type of temple was produced by the number and prominence of its pillars and piers, and the manner in which they were sculpted into the most complicated positions, strange and manifold, so that each becomes a figurative drama in stone.[10]

Coomaraswamy, writing mainly on the Vithala temple, attempts to summarise the important features of Vijayanagara sculpture and concentrates on the analysis of the pillars which are one of its main characteristic components: 'The pillar caryatids, whether rearing lions or yalis (gaja-simhas) are products of a wild phantasy...'.[11] Rowland expands on the Vithala temple, noting especially the pillared hall and the sculptural quality of the piers: 'Each one of these piers is really a complete sculptured group rather than an architectural order...'. Speaking of the famous horse court at Srirangam, Rowland stresses that:

> These charging cavaliers are in a sense the final fantastic evolution from the column supported by a rampant animal which begins in Pallava architecture. It here attains an extravagance that has an inevitable suggestion of the grotesque and fanciful quality of some European medieval art...
>
> The precision and sharpness with which the highly polished chlorite stone is carved into the most fantastic and baroque entanglements of figures almost make it appear as though they were wrought in cast steel, rather than stone.[12]

The above quotations demonstrate that when writing on Vijayanagara art, the various authors' attention was generally drawn to its late and most spectacular phase; particularly as the only temple mentioned is the Vithala (more precisely its pillared mandapas which are a mid-sixteenth-century addition to the complex): and moreover they dwell on the monuments at Srirangam and at Kanchipuram, which are more accessible than the monuments at the capital.

Passages like 'the grotesque and fanciful quality of some European medieval art...' and 'baroque entanglements of figures' show how, as late as the end of the 1950s, Western art historians were still assessing Indian aesthetics according to European standards. Such quotations reflect the general attitude of Western scholars, who did not seem to appreciate the different aesthetic norms of Indian art. One suspects that such scholars never had an opportunity to visit Vijayanagara and study the monuments in situ. All the descriptions quoted concentrate on the exquisite workmanship of the pieces but nothing is mentioned about what is actually represented. It seems likely that most of such scholarly contributions were the result of the use of woodcuts and photographs, which did not enable them to identify the sculptures, and also inhibited actual aesthetic appreciation. Furthermore, the earlier work at the capital was ignored.

Among the early art historians only Fergusson (1876) and Longhurst (1917) deal in detail with the main monuments at Vijayanagara, especially, again, the Vithala temple. Moreover, Fergusson includes in his discussion of Vijayanagara architecture the two temples at Tadapatri and the palace at Chandragiri. Thus the situation remained until Devakunjari published her guidebook in 1970.[13] The situation changed dramatically at the beginning of the 1980s when the publications of John Fritz, George Michell and other members of the Vijayanagara Research Project brought the site to the forefront of art-historical research. The subsequent surveys of Indian art by S. and J. Huntingdon (1985) and J.C. Harle (1986) each devote a chapter to Vijayanagara art.[14] The most recent study in the field is George Michell's *Architecture and Art of Southern India: Vijayanagara and the Successor States* (Cambridge, 1995). This comprehensive survey of the art of southern India assesses the seminal importance of Vijayanagara art, both at the capital and throughout the region.

The response to Vijayanagara art, especially sculpture, moves dramatically from reticent approval to genuine enthusiasm when the writings of Indian scholars are examined. An important example is Saletore, who is one of the few who actually visited the site. Saletore (1936) was perhaps the first scholar to write with fervour on the sculptures of the Vijayanagara period:

> On the walls of temples or of other buildings was displayed the sculpture of the Vijayanagara craftsmen. Probably in the whole range of South Indian sculpture it would be difficult to find a match to vie with the variety of Vijayanagara sculpture. In order to prove this one should go primarily to Vijayanagara not to mention Srisailam, Vellore or Mudabidri or even Bhatkal, where are unravelled in stone a social history of this age.... The obvious heaviness of Hoysala sculptures, especially of the horses, for instance, which one notices at Halebid or at Dvarasamudra, is conspicuous by its absence in Vijayanagara sculpture of this period. The deer, the dogs, the prancing horses or the marching soldiers look alive, instinct with life, vigour and freshness which are unforgettable.[15]

Much later, Sivaramamurti (1961) draws attention to the narrative friezes decorating the walls of the Ramachandra temple at the capital, and also to the panels showing scenes from the Ramayana and the Bhagavata Purana on the 'Vishnu' temple at Penukonda, noting a similar treatment of Shaiva subjects on the walls of the adjacent Shiva temple. It is again Sivaramamurti who mentions the art of portraiture in

Vijayanagara sculpture as one of the main achievements of the time, in particular the images of Krishnadevaraya and his queens at Tirumala, and of the same king at Chidambaram.[16]

In order to arrive at a satisfactory aesthetic assessment of southern Indian art from the sixteenth century onwards, it is necessary to understand the artistic development at Vijayanagara. As all previous works give only fragmentary information regarding Vijayanagara sculpture, systematic study of this whole subject has yet to be made.[17]

In any such study the physical setting of Vijayanagara must first be considered. The town is situated in a dramatic landscape amid rocky hills and granite outcrops through which the river Tungabhadra flows. This region, according to a long-lasting tradition, is linked to the god Rama and particularly with the Kishkindha book of the Ramayana. Caves, ponds, rocks and summits of hills are believed to be the locations of specific incidents of the Ramayana.

The mapping of the site, undertaken in recent years by the team of John Fritz and George Michell, has demonstrated that several of the city's structures were aligned with these natural features. Thus, it is evident that there was a conscious effort to link spatially the world of the king with that of Rama. Not only was the landscape mythologically charged with the presence of Rama, the king himself was occasionally compared with this god, and similarly a comparison was made between the capital and Ayodhya (an inscription of 1379 declares: 'In the same city did Harihara dwell, as in former times Rama dwelt in...the city of Ayodhya'). Furthermore, the king was ritually identified with Rama in the Mahanavami festival, a spectacular nine-day ceremony which commemorated the worship of the goddess Durga by Rama on the eve of the decisive battle against Ravana. As demonstrated by Fritz and Michell:

> Vijayanagara was the urban realization of cosmological principles which infused the ruler with divine power. When political and military success combined with sacred authority, the king and his capital came to have an epic, almost mythical dimension.[18]

From such a mythological background, there developed a specific aesthetic. However, within this chapter it is only possible to highlight some significant aspects of the matter and to attempt some tentative conclusions.

The artistic activity at Vijayanagara was closely associated with the dynasties which ruled the empire from circa 1336 up to 1565: the Sangamas from the second half of the fourteenth century until the last decade of the fifteenth, the Saluvas from circa 1489 until 1501, and the

Tuluvas from 1505 to 1568. The vast extent of the territory which constituted the Vijayanagara empire—from the Arabian Sea to the Bay of Bengal across the Deccan plateau and south India—has to be kept in mind. All these domains had once been the strongholds of renowned dynasties such as the Chalukyas (early and late), the Hoysalas, the Cholas and the Pandyas. Because of this varied artistic heritage the early phase of art activity at Vijayanagara follows two distinct styles, one influenced by the Deccan tradition and the other by the Tamil. By the beginning of the fifteenth century, the former was abandoned in favour of the latter. With the Tuluvas, it is possible to speak of an 'imperial style' of building. There is a standardisation of design and of building techniques which facilitated temple construction, so that, while temples became larger and more complex in their overall layout, they became increasingly similar. An important element in the assessment of Vijayanagara art is its dissemination throughout the imperial territory: for the local governors, even in the remotest parts of the empire, tried, sometimes very successfully, to emulate the imperial style and, in the process, local idioms were evolved.

The last dynasty, the Aravidus (1569-1674) who came to power after the destruction of Vijayanagara, governed from Chandragiri. They patronised building projects at the nearby temple of Tirumala, and at Tirupati, as well as in the Tamil territory immediately to the south under the control of Vellore.

Most of these dynasties had, as far as artistic work was concerned, definite predilections regarding the sculptural themes. During some two centuries, when Vijayanagara was the capital of the homonymous empire, there is a marked shift in the interest of the patrons, whether kingly personages or members of the nobility or the army, from martial and courtly scenes to the depiction of mythological and religious themes. This chapter focuses on some of the themes which were evolved during this period.

Narrative sculpture

The first major sculptural works at the capital are the narrative friezes on the multi-storeyed Mahanavami platform in the royal centre at Vijayanagara which is very important for several reasons. First of all it is the oldest example of 'narrative art' at the site, and, more significantly, the throne platform imagery is exclusively royal in character. In spite of the general preference shown by artists and patrons for the representations of gods and goddesses, not one divine image is to be found among the reliefs carved on its sides (Figs 1, 2).

Fig. 1 Mahanavami platform, south side: military parades and hunting scenes

Fig. 2 Mahanavami platform, south side: hunting scenes

As in the majority of the monuments at the site, the material used is granite. The reliefs are carved in a vigorous and expressionistic style in shallow relief on individual blocks of different sizes, according to their positioning on the monument. This powerful, unrestrained style takes one back to the second half of the fourteenth century when this part of the capital was laid out. There is no immediately recognisable sculptural programme, although this possibility cannot be excluded at this stage of enquiry. The courtly themes on this monument are seminal for the appreciation and understanding of most of the non-sacred themes found on basement friezes, column blocks and piers in the later phases of Vijayanagara art at the capital, which are developed in southern Indian sculpture of the seventeenth and eighteenth centuries.

The style of the carvings in the oldest phase of this monument, where the granite is sculpted in a very shallow relief—almost 'flattened'—has puzzled various scholars. Sharp, angular movements often characterise the figures constituting these friezes. Goetz wrote on the origin of Vijayanagara art as follows:

> The indigenous sculpture of Vijayanagar developed from the style of the funeral steles (virakkal and satikkal) and snake stone of Western Calukyan times. Their representation is naive, in flat stripes, without foreshortening or perspective but immensely vital.[19]

Michell stresses this point more precisely, analysing the style and iconography of the memorial stones:

> Despite their limited iconographic schemes, memorial stones may be considered relevant to the sculptures on the great platform at Vijayanagara in two ways. (1) Memorial stones are carved in granite in a robust and somewhat crude style, sometimes emphasising the animated posture of warriors and fighters. (2) As their central theme, memorials stress the heroic actions of brave and pious men, not gods. Both in style and purpose, these commemorative folk monuments are far removed from temple art.[20]

A further example of royal imagery as the only theme of a set of carvings—possibly of the parades of the Mahanavami festival, so much admired and vividly described by the foreign visitors in the fifteenth and sixteenth centuries—is seen on the outer compound wall of the Ramachandra temple (Fig. 3), a short distance from the Mahanavami throne platform. These carvings, more restrained in style and carefully finished, are organised according to a very clear arrangement: the bottom row is occupied by elephants either uprooting trees or lifting foliage; the second row shows an unending parade of splendidly caparisoned horses led by outlandish grooms; the third row is a

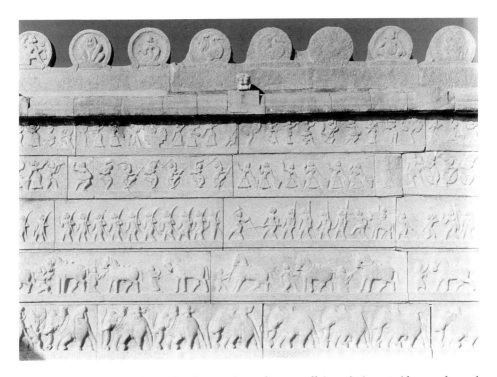

Fig. 3 Ramachandra temple, enclosure wall (exterior), east side: parades and dancing scenes

celebration of sports and military parades; the fourth and fifth rows are reserved for female dancers and musicians and the celebration of the Vasantotsava—the spring festival—one of the major annual events at Vijayanagara. All these men, women and animals proceed in an uninterrupted clockwise sequence around the monument, starting from the southwestern corner of the complex and ending at the main gateway in the east. At various intervals royal figures and noblemen, mounted on horses and shaded by parasols, or seated in elegant slender-pillared pavilions with their entourage, either inspect the troops or enjoy the musical and dance performances.

The Mahanavami platform and these last-mentioned carvings are the only two outstanding examples of royal narrative at Vijayanagara, both attributable to the Sangama era. In these two monuments the royal personages appear in a formal setting; generally seated, accompanied by retainers and guards, intently watching parades and dance performances, or receiving traders from far-away countries. Their staticity contrasts with the movement which surrounds them.

The royal theme, although ever present, is never again so extensively and conspicuously treated. In the sixteenth century, processions of horses, elephants, dancers, musicians and warriors are relegated to basements, cornices and pillar blocks, while the rearing tigers of the hunting episodes, and the rearing horses of the parade scenes, are developed and transformed into the spectacular and highly sophisticated yalis which adorn piers and columns, and which became one of the characteristics of Nayaka sculpture.

The royal theme is gradually replaced by mythological ones; for example, two early sets of Ramayana sculptures are carved on the outer walls of the main shrine, and on part of the inner face of the enclosure wall, of the Ramachandra temple (Figs 4, 5).

The Ramachandra temple can be definitely assigned to the early fifteenth century (Devaraya I, 1406-1422) on the basis of epigraphical evidence. From the early fifteenth century onwards, the cult of Rama gained in popularity and enjoyed the patronage of the court as well as support from the masses. As stated before, a homology was established between Rama, the universal king and his human counterpart, the Raya. So much so that, when depicting Rama on the pillars of this and other temples, the sculptors resorted to an intentional ambiguity in order, perhaps, to draw a parallel between the divine and earthly kings. This temple, which constitutes the nucleus of the 'royal centre' and whose importance in the urban context and symbolic layout of the capital has been highlighted by Michell and Fritz[21] contains three important sets of carvings of which the Ramayana narratives on the walls of the principal shrine and on the enclosure wall are the most outstanding.

A set of 108 panels proceeds in a clockwise sequence in three tiers around the outer walls of the principal shrine. Each panel, generally enclosed in a makara-torana, has a restricted number of figures, generally two or three, and the artist compresses the climax of a single episode into each panel. The figures, imitating the Tamil idiom, are sculpted in high relief with great attention given to the rendering of costumes, head-dress and jewellery. The panels are arranged in such a way that the six sections of the story are spatially separated, beginning or ending at the north and south porches. Crucial events tend to be placed at the cardinal points and at the corners of the building, and there are ingenious spatial relationships linking the various panels.[22]

The second set of Ramayana carvings covers part of the inner face of the enclosure wall. It proceeds in five rows beginning on the eastern side of the north gateway, where the story of Shravanakumara is narrated as a prologue to the story, and ends at the east and main

Fig. 4 Ramachandra temple, principal shrine, south side: Ramayana reliefs

Fig. 5 Ramachandra temple, enclosure wall (interior), north side: Ramayana reliefs

gateway. While the first four rows proceed from north to east, the sequence of the fifth row is reversed.

Throughout, the carving is vigorous. Characteristic of this series is the depiction of movement. Landscape elements are used with great inventiveness; for instance, trees subdivide the panels, creating separate spaces for successive episodes. Architecture, even when reduced to merely conventional elements, serves to define the figures indicating their place or urban context by the simplest means. Very frequently the narrative overlaps the panels: characters in one panel often look backwards or forwards to adjacent panels. In this manner, the sculptural compositions are directed towards propelling the story to its inevitable climax.

The sculptural style of the two series is very different. The one on the enclosure wall recalls, by its vitality and power of expression, the carvings on the throne platform. Here the staticity of the set of sculptures adorning the principal shrine is replaced by action. A possible explanation for this diversity in style is perhaps to be found in the sizes of the stone blocks (circa 80 cm in height and 3 metres in length) and the absence of architectural elements between which the scenes had to be fitted. The carving technique is also different: the series on the principal shrine is in a bold, rounder relief, the one on the enclosure wall is 'flattened'. There is a striking parallel between the carvings on the enclosure wall of the Ramachandra temple and the ones on the outer wall of the Sri Mallikarjuna temple at Srisailam, which is datable to the same period, and was patronised by the Sangamas.

From the late fifteenth century onwards, narrative reliefs on such an ambitious scale are no longer in vogue at the capital and, except for a few examples like the Uttara-Ramayana depicted on the walls of the 'subsidiary shrine' in the Ramachandra temple complex and the Ramayana set on the entrance gopura of the so-called 'Old Shiva' temple, the narratives are generally reduced in size so as to fit around a pillar (i.e., a maximum of twelve panels).

This sculptural genre, however, which is one of the inventions of Vijayanagara artists, continued to be popular outside the capital for a long time. It suffices to mention here only two examples from two different parts of the empire: in the Telugu zone, the splendid Ramayana and Bhagavata relief series depicted on the walls of the Chintala Venkataramana temple at Tadapatri (mix-sixteenth century), and the Ramayana reliefs of the Khetapai Narayana temple at Bhatkal in the Kannada zone (seventeenth century). Moreover, narrative reliefs are frequently found in the gopuras, such as at the sixteenth-century

Ventakaramana temple in Gingee, and the Sri Govindaraja temple at Tirupati (of 1624).

The focus of sculptural activity shifts from temple and enclosure walls to the open pillared halls designed for the celebration of various rituals, and to the colonnades skirting the courtyard's walls. This gave ample scope to the artist (master-designer or patron) to develop a set of variations on the simple three-square block column which had been widely used until this period. The outer piers of these pillared halls became elaborate sculptural compositions in their own right,

Fig. 6 Vithala temple: yali and composite pillar

surrounded by clusters of colonnettes carved out of a single block and supported by crouching yalis. Full-scale leaping yalis with diminutive riders are reserved for the piers in the middle of each side (Fig. 6). This type of column was then to be elaborated upon subsequently, especially in the Tamil area.

The emphasis in building projects is now on size and complexity of overall planning. The temples built or enlarged in the course of the sixteenth century testify to this development (for example, the new pillared halls built in the Vithala temple, new temples like the Krishna temple of 1515, and the Tiruvengalanatha of 1534). By this time, Vijayanagara was not only a cosmic city governed by a ruler closely linked to Rama, but also a ceremonial capital, and last but not least one of the wealthiest cities in the world. The scale of the buildings and their bold style of sculpture are witness to this. The figures are no longer flattened or in shallow relief, but emerge boldly from the stone; moreover, in the complex compositions adorning the piers of the pillared halls the figures are carved in the round.

Iconographic repertoire on columns

The themes sculpted on the column blocks cover a wide repertoire. Among the usual depictions of gods and goddesses in their various aspects, animals, musicians, dancers, and ascetics, there are two innovations: kingly figures and icons related to special pilgrimage centres.

Kingly figures are sculpted on the sides of the throne platform, and in the reliefs on the outer enclosure wall of the Ramachandra temple, but none of these can be identified with any of the Rayas. The only clearly identified royal portrait before the sixteenth century is that of King Mallikarjuna (1446-1465) at the entrance to the sanctum of the Anjaneya temple. In the sixteenth century, royal figures are more frequent. They are found on pillars: in the Krishna temple, a kingly figure, locally identified as Krishnadevaraya, is depicted once worshipping the linga (Fig. 7), and once worshipping Balakrishna. In the Virupaksha temple, in the passage leading to the Manmatha Honda, again a kingly figure, inscribed 'Rayalu'—locally identified with Krishnadevaraya—stands with hands in *anjali mudra*.

It should be noted that clearly identifiable kingly portraits are found outside the capital; it may suffice to mention here the superb bronze portraits of Krishnadevaraya and his queens in the Sri Venkateshvara temple at Tirumala, and the sculpture in the round in the north gopura of the Chidambaram temple.

Fig. 7 Krishna temple, porch pillar (detail): royal figure worshipping the linga
(photo courtesy of Anila Verghese)

In the Tiruvengalanatha temple, a kingly figure, perhaps Achyuta
Raya's brother-in-law, Hiriya Tirumala, who was the patron of the
temple, is repeatedly depicted on pillars in the Amman shrine. Here are
possibly the humble beginnings of the spectacular galleries of portraits
which grace the Nayaka temples of the later centuries.

The royal figures at worship lead to the next important theme which
emerges during this time: the mythology related to a holy place
(*sthalapurana*) becomes a very popular subject in sculpture, and more
especially in painting.

The first experiment, in the sculptural rendering of a *sthalapurana*,
is found on the bottom register of the throne platform, on the southern
side. Here, disguised among the various hunting scenes, is a sequence
showing a huntress leaning on a bow and a hunter extracting a thorn

from her foot. This scene became in the later decades the iconographic formula condensing the foundation story of the temple at Ahobilam, when Narasimha roaming through the forests fell in love with a Chenchu girl whom, after many trials, he eventually married. This episode is repeated twice on the throne platform (both sequences are to be found on the same register) and it is known that there was a connection between the Sangamas and their successors and the Ahobilam temple.

Images related to well-known pilgrimage places became increasingly popular. Pandharpur is referred to by the image of Vitthala standing upright with the arms resting on the hips (a good example is found on the west side of the small southern entrance to the Ramachandra temple complex). Venkateshvara—a reference to Tirumala—is depicted very frequently at the site, especially from the late fifteenth century. Kanchipuram is signified by Varadaraja-Vishnu freeing the elephant from the crocodile; and Kalahasti by the Shaiva saint Kannappa plucking out his eyes.

The Vijayanagara Rayas had established religious and political ties with these major centres of worship which they regularly visited, and to which they sent substantial donations. Images of saints, like Kannappa, but more frequently the Vaishnava Alvars, appear on the pillars of temples at the capital in the sixteenth century (Figs 8, 9).

In brief, the sculptural programme for the pillars of the sixteenth-century *mandapas* and cloisters is not merely inspired by religious piety, but also by political acumen. This is typified by the portraits of Krishnadevaraya in the Krishna temple. As mentioned before, in one of the carvings the king is shown worshipping Balakrishna, the god whose image he had captured in the siege of Udayagiri and for whom he had built the temple; in the other he is shown worshipping the age-old tutelary deity of Vijayanagara, Virupaksha.

The Vijayanagara empire, never a highly centralised state, but, in the words of Burton Stein, a 'segmentary state', relied on the military and financial support of the representatives of the Raya (not necessarily his relatives) who ruled the various territories.[23] Behind the extensive patronage which the Rayas bestowed on the various pilgrimage centres—some of them in extremely remote areas, such as Ahobilam and Sringeri—there were strategical and commercial interests, such as the safeguarding of the access to the Bay of Bengal and to the Arabian Sea. In order to please the various local rulers, their deities were displayed and worshipped at the capital.

Fig. 8 Virupaksha temple, porch pillar (detail): Kannappa plucking out his eye

There is another theme which was widely developed at Vijayanagara: everyday life. Saletore first mentioned the vast repertoire of motifs displayed on the walls and pillars of the monuments of this epoch.[24] The range of the subjects depicted and the unconventional treatment they received at the hands of the artists—generally dubbed 'crude'—are perhaps the reason why this remarkable sculpture has not been sufficiently appreciated. Vijayanagara sculpture is the expression of a different and new spirit: never before have secular, everyday scenes, such as courtly life, processions, kingly figures, animals, birds and yalis been so frequently represented in temple sculpture. There is a clear shifting of focus. It is not only the world of the gods and of the heroes which constitutes the theme of the carvings, but there is an unmistakable interest in the rendering of everyday activities (Fig 10).

Fig. 9 Virupaksha temple, porch pillar (detail); Narasimha extracting a thorn from the foot of the Chenchu Lakshmi

Vignettes depicting everyday life are encountered in works dating from earlier times, such as the depiction of hunters, peasants and water-carriers on the relief of 'Arjuna's Penance' at Mamallapuram. Secular scenes are detected on the carved friezes along the base of the Hoysala period temples at Belur and Halebid. In these cases, however, the impression is that the depiction of 'secular scenes' is only accessory. In the reliefs at Vijayanagara, on the other hand, the everyday world plays a more dominant role. This originates from the very beginning of Vijayanagara sculpture, that is from the reliefs on the throne platform.

Conclusion

In the light of what as been said, when discussing the art of a given period, the contemporary aesthetic system should not be overlooked. When Vijayanagara is studied it is particularly fortunate that this city, albeit in ruins, is still extant and a wealth of epigraphical and historical information is available. This occasionally helps dating and clarifying the occasion when a given monument was built. Since Vijayanagara was not constructed in a historical vacuum, the antecedents of the Vijayanagara style have also to be taken into account.

At the beginning there does not seem to have been an overall aesthetic principle determining the artistic creativity at Vijayanagara. The general impression is that, in the early decades when Vijayanagara was the capital of the empire, there was not yet one uniform style but rather many styles which co-existed. The two more obvious are the archaic, used mainly in cult images—bronzes are a very good example since stone cult images are still used in worship and difficult to examine—echoing the great Tamil tradition of the Cholas and the Pandyas, and the autochthonous Deccan style originating in the memorial stones.

An example of the co-existence of both styles is seen in the Ramachandra temple complex: the archaic manner appears in the Ramayana carvings on the walls of the principal shrine, where deeply-cut small-sized compositions are enclosed in elaborate makara toranas; in contrast is the Ramayana series on the enclosure wall which exemplifies the uninhibited, vigorous style, having its antecedents in the carvings of the throne platform and in the memorial stones.

With the advent of the sixteenth century, changes come about and a 'Vijayanagara style' gradually beings to emerge. The focus of artistic activity shifts to ambitious architectural projects. Because of the tremendous output, much of the pillar sculpture is of a standard quality.

Fig. 10 Ramachandra temple, east gateway: huntress

The quality of the carving, however, was not important. The pillars
were coated with a thin plaster film which evened the rough carvings
and added to details of costume and jewellery barely hewn in the stone
before being painted: traces of the pristine beautifying coat of paint is
still, though rarely, visible.

From the accession of Krishnadevaraya, when the power of the
empire was at its zenith, there was a conscious effort to attempt to co-
ordinate the various diffused artistic traditions spanning more than a
century and to create a new style. This is immediately recognisable in:
(1) the monumentality of proportions—irrespective of whether it was
an architectural or sculptural project: the 1528 Ugra-Narasimha
monolith, 6.7 metres high, and its smaller neighbours—the two
Ganeshas—on the ridge immediately above Hampi, are good examples;
(2) the concern for overall planning: this is especially true of
architectural projects such as the Tiruvengalanatha temple of 1534; (3)
the layout of ceremonial streets with colonnades sometimes provided
with parapets decorated with exquisite plasterwork, such as Virupaksha
bazaar; (4) the building and stucco decoration of gopuras; (5) the
addition of ceremonial mandapas, hundred-pillared halls, cloisters and
corridors to temples contributing to the coalescence of sculpture and

architecture: fully-modelled figures and animals support mandapa roofs—the first experiment is the 1510 open pillared hall of the Virupaksha temple followed, at a later point, by the superb open mandapas of the Vitthala temple; (6) a new dimension in animal themes, with the development of the rearing yalis and horses with armed riders jumping, as it were, out of the piers; (7) the new iconographies, introducing elements from other parts of the empire; (8) the portrayal of kings and noblemen as patrons of religious establishments; and (9) the depiction of scenes from daily life.

All these stylistic elements, 'invented' at Vijayanagara, cannot be appreciated if analysed apart from the historical religious and social contexts, or from their specific purposes: be it the glorification of the king/god Rama, or the desire to integrate new religious cults. In the course of the centuries, the Vijayanagara inspiration was disseminated throughout southern India, contributing to most imposing and exquisite works of art. Some of the Vijayanagara stylistic features were altered to suit regional tastes, at other times they were discarded and later rediscovered. Still in the twentieth century, from Australia to California, Hindu temples are built according to the Dravidian style, which, in other words, means a mixture of Vijayanagara and Nayaka styles.

[1] E. Löschhorn, 'Vijayanagara as seen by European visitors' in A.L. Dallapiccola and S. Singel-Avé Lallemant (eds.), *Vijayanagara City and Empire: new currents of research*, 2 vols. (Wiesbaden, 1985), pp.344-53, p.344.

[2] R. Sewell (1970), p.86.

[3] Löschhorn, 'Vijayanagara as seen by European visitors', p.345.

[4] Sewell, pp.247-8.

[5] Ibid, pp.250-1.

[6] Ibid., p.245

[7] J.C. Mardrus (trans.), *Les Mille et Une Nuits*, 16 vols. (Paris, 1904), vol.XII, pp.288ff..

[8] A. Rea, quoted in R.N. Saletore, *Vijayanagara Art* (Delhi, 1982), p.52..

[9] Vincent Smith, *History of Fine Art in India and Ceylon* (Oxford, 1911), p.52.

[10] Percy Brown, *Indian Architecture (Hindu and Buddhist Periods)*, 5th edn. (Bombay, 1965), p.91

[11] A.K. Coomaraswamy, *History of Indian and Indonesian Art* (New York, 1965 (1927)), p.124.

[12] Benjamin Rowland, *The Art and Architecture of India* (Harmondsworth, 1959), p.181.

[13] J. Fergusson, *History of Indian and Eastern Architecture*, 2 vols. (London, 1876); A.H. Longhurst, *Hampi Ruins Described and Illustrated* (London, 1917); D. Devankunjari, *Hampi* (New Delhi, 1970).

[14] S. and J. Huntingdon, *The Art of Ancient India* (1985); J.C. Harle, *The Art and Architecture of the Indian Subcontinent* (Harmondsworth, 1986)

[15] R.N. Saletore, 'Some aspects of art during the reign of Krishnadevaraya the Great', in *Vijayanagara Sexcentenary Commemoration Volume* (Dharwad, 1936), pp.197-206, p.202..

[16] C. Sivaramamurti, *Indian Sculpture* (New Delhi, 1961), pp.134, 174, 288.

[17] A volume by Dallapiccola and Verghese is in press.

[18] J. Gollings, J.M. Fritz and G, Michell, *City of Victory, Vijayanagara* (New York, 1991), p.11. See also G. Michell, *The Vijayanagara Courtly Style* (New Delhi, 1991), and G. Michell, *Architecture and Art of Vijayanagara and the Successor States* (Cambridge, forthcoming).

[19] Herman Goetz (1959), quoted in Saletore, *Vijayanagara Art*, p.130.

[20] G. Michell, 'Folk traditions in a monumental setting: sculptures on the Great Platform at Vijayanagara', in L. Chandra and J. Jain (eds.), *Dimensions of Indian Art* (Delhi, 1986), pp.287-90, p.289..

[21] J. Fritz, G. Michell and M.S. Nagaraja Rao, *Where Kings and Gods Meet: the royal centre at Vijayanagara* (Tucson, 1984), pp.149-54.

[22] A.L. Dallapiccola, J. Fritz, G. Michell and S. Rajasekhara, *The Ramachandra Temple at Vijayanagara* (New Delhi, 1992), pp.92-3.

[23] Burton Stein, *The New Cambridge History of India*: 1.2: *Vijayanagara* (Cambridge, 1989) p. xii.

[24] Saletore, 'Some aspects of art', p.202.

Chapter Seven

SPATIAL ORGANISATION AND AESTHETIC EXPRESSION IN THE TRADITIONAL ARCHITECTURE OF RAJASTHAN

Kulbhushan Jain

Indian architecture conjures up an image of large monuments like the Taj Mahal, religious complexes like the temples of the south and, in its uniqueness, the cave architecture of Ajanta and Ellora. It also brings to mind impressions of the mud houses of rural India. By and large, the urban architecture of the common people fails to ring that kind of bell. Although the traditional urban architecture has been rich and worth looking at, most of it has been lost either to neglect or to commercial exploitation, though there may be some justification on account of the 'need of the hour'. However, one can still find many examples of traditional wooden architecture in Gujarat, brick and wood buildings in the south and outstanding stone houses in Rajasthan. In today's context, we can learn much from these traditions without trying to imitate the buildings.

This chapter is based on the understanding gained through studies of traditional urban architecture in Rajasthan. As is clear from the topic of the chapter, this presentation is specific and confined to those aspects related to the organisation of spaces and related aesthetic expression in the traditional architecture of Rajasthan. There are several other aspects of art forms which have also contributed to the rich traditions in this region, but they are not included here.

Rajasthan is the 'land of kingdoms'. Andrew Topsfield sums it up well:

> The Rajputs, 'sons of kings', had originally entered India from the north-west during the first millennium A.D. They established kingdoms in western India in a region that came to be called Rajasthan, 'the abode of kings'. Like previous immigrants from Central Asia, they were assimilated into the all-embracing Hindu social system as Kshatriyas or members of the warrior caste. When northern India fell under the domination of Muslim Turks from the 13th century onwards, the Rajputs were foremost in resisting the alien invaders and in preserving the surviving traditions of classical Hindu culture at their courts. They have been proverbial in India since those days for their courage, tending to recklessness, and for their code of honour and chivalry. Many heroic legends from Rajput folklore

Fig. 1 A house in Chauganpura, in the fort of Jaisalmer

are recounted by James Tod, the first British Political Agent in Mewar (1818-22) and author of a classic history....[1]

Rajasthan is not an area of geo-political delineations only, but also an area of distinct cultural expression. The state also has some unique geographical characteristics, though the entire region does not show the same physical attributes. However, there are cultural and aesthetic expressions which can be identified as distinct and belonging to this cultural entity. There are social values and customs which find expression in the life-style, costumes and architecture. It is interesting to see how an element like the *zharookha* carries the same significance as the *ghoonghat* (veil). In both cases the privacy of women and their selective participation with the outside world are expressed (Fig. 1).

One very interesting aspect of the values people cherish is expressed through two words: *Geet aur Bheet*—meaning the song and the wall. Both these signify the notion of celebration. In Rajasthan all occasions of joy are celebrated with singing and therefore song has a special meaning. Secondly, the *Bheet*, meaning the wall, signifies construction or house-building. This is another very important aspect of the culture. People spend much of their wealth in celebrations and building homes. This has led to extraordinary effort in the building of houses.

I would like to divide the subject into three basic parts dealing with a variety of aspects. First, I shall examine the spatial organisation of traditional urban architecture in Rajasthan. The discussion is not specific to one or two case studies, but attempts to capture the essence which can be perceived throughout the state, with some variations. In spite of differences in local contextual conditions such as climate and topography, there is a basic commonality in the organisation of spaces. It is this essence of the commonality that we are attempting to understand. The second part deals with that aspect of architecture where the structural organisation and the aesthetic expression are mutually dependent, at least in their origin. It means that there is a basic logic in the creation of architecture, and it is this logic that leads to the visual qualities of the built form. The primary aspects of architectural organisation also determine the aesthetics of the building. In other words, the structural system determines the expression of the building. Here the determinant and the form are inseparable—an attitude which has universal value and is also the basis of modern architecture. More importantly, this determinant to form relationship is clearly perceived.

In the third section of the chapter, the attempt is to identify and study those aesthetic expressions which are independent of the basic

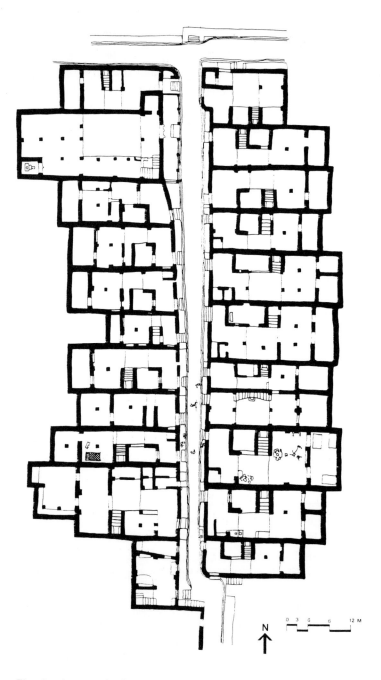

Fig. 2   A street in Jaisalmer; the social distribution determinant is the community group rather than economic status

Fig. 3 Brahmapuri, a street in Jodhpur; all the inhabitants are from the Brahmin community, irrespective of economic status, resulting in the juxtaposition of large and small houses.

logic of form-making. They do not conform to any predetermined architectural attitude. As a matter of fact, architectural elements, or images of the elements, are freely used to provide grounds for other visual treatment.

Spatial organisation

As in several other places, the spatial organisation of the traditional architecture of this region has responded well to the constraints imposed by nature on the one hand and the interpersonal relationships of the people on the other. These constraints are generally well accepted as principal determinants. They include: function and privacy relationships; climate, topography and land form; and local materials and construction methods. Simple rectilinear geometry is used as a tool for organising various spaces and for sequencing movement and establishing zones of different grades of privacy. This has resulted in a hierarchical pattern in most of the dwelling structures.

Most houses, irrespective of their size, in the towns and cities of Rajasthan form part of a well-defined street system (Figs 2, 3). This means that a very large *haveli* and a very small house can co-exist next to each other and still be able to present a harmonious facade. These urban houses always share their side walls, which are often the longer ones, in narrow and deep houses. This results in a continuous facade with some variation in the height of the houses. Therefore, one observes a very strong relationship between a house and the street; the connection is also very important. There is an elaborate effort to make a threshold which signifies several things. It is more than just an entry to the house.

The idea of the threshold always had a special significance in the cultural milieu of the Indian people, and Rajasthan is no exception. It has been symbolised in several ways—in religious rituals, in mythology, in paintings and in literature. Not only in its manifestations as a physical entity on the edge of a town or a city, or as an entrance to a house, the idea extended to the in-between realms such as the dawn or the dusk or the land-water interface. So, many of the activities and rituals are connected with the mornings and the evenings—the transitions between day and night. Traditionally the houses always had a threshold, whether it was a small wooden one which formed part of the door frame, or an extended one which could be large enough to accommodate certain activities. Several rituals and sentiments were always associated with the idea of crossing the threshold, one way or the other. This resulted in an extra effort to define and express the element of entry to a house. Alcoves for lamps and auspicious symbols were integrated into this element (Figs 4, 5).

Since the central portion of a house is always quite open, it became necessary to block the view for anyone entering the house. A baffle

Fig. 4 Street-house connection in Udaipur; the ground floor of the house is used as a workshop

Fig. 5 Entrance to a house in Udaipur; note the auspicious hand symbol

wall is used in front of the entrance door, and one is forced to turn around for entry. The element so created is called a *modh*. The central open courtyard is called the *chowk*, and its surrounding area is the *parsal*. In the sequence of spatial organisation, a *chowk* is an extremely important element. Efforts are made to make internal facades as elaborate as the ones outside, and the courtyard is normally a very

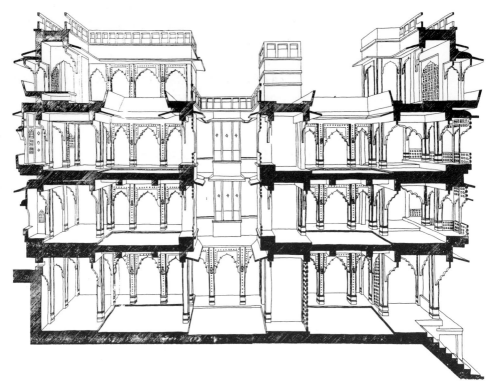

Fig. 6 Sectional view of a haveli in Jaisalmer

beautiful part of a house. This space connects other spaces not only horizontally but even vertically. Privacy notions are also applicable here. The views, particularly on upper residential floors, are always controlled and one cannot look across. However, the presence of *zharookhas* overlooking the courtyard, gives a choice to the inhabitants to participate visually in the activities in the other parts of the house. Interestingly, major portions of a house have a name and an identity which are not based strictly on function (Figs 6, 7).

The spatial organisation of the upper floors accommodates more private functions like sleeping. Most of the spaces continue to draw their sustenance from the courtyard. Houses start opening out more as one moves up. The ground-level is invariably very closed to the street, except for the threshold. The privacy needs are obviously far greater at the public level than at the upper levels. Just like the courtyard, there are terraces at various levels of the houses. These terraces are almost like courtyards at different floor levels, since they are designed spaces and not left-out roofs. A sense of enclosure is created to add to the quality of space. It also provides greater privacy and therefore finds greater use. All this also adds much richness to the visual quality of architecture. Here the terraces are design opportunities and therefore much is expressed through them.

The climate of Rajasthan is essentially hot and dry. A major part of the state is actually a desert. It is normal to experience hot, unbearable and long summer days. At the same time, late evenings and mornings

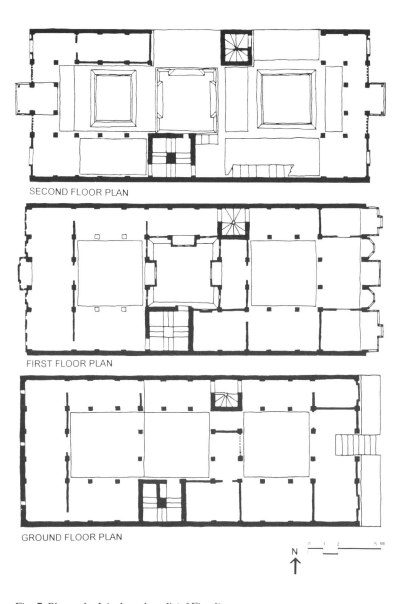

SECOND FLOOR PLAN

FIRST FLOOR PLAN

GROUND FLOOR PLAN

Fig. 7 Plans of a Jaisalmer haveli (cf Fig. 6)

are pleasant. Nights can actually be quite cool. Also, within the state of Rajasthan, there are strong climatic differences, as between Jaisalmer and Udaipur, yet one can find similarities in the architectural expression of such places. Builders in Rajasthan were obviously responding to such contrasting conditions and they created spaces and elements responding to activities. They made beautiful courtyards, terraces *zharookhas* and other places in houses. Not only do they provide for the harsh climatic conditions, but also respond well to the needs of an introverted life-style.

You are drawn outdoors for several activities, particularly during the morning and evening hours, essentially for climatic reasons; and in winter, even during the daytime when the warmth of the sun is welcome. At the same time, a sense of enclosure, a sense of space and a very strong need for privacy created semi-covered and open enclosures. It was desirable that one should be outdoors and still retain one's privacy. As can be seen in the illustrations, the effort expended in making such elements, which relate the house to the outside, is considerable. The elements so generated can be enumerated as: thresholds, *zharookhas, parsals,* courtyards, balconies, terraces, cupolas etc. These elements have often been used as a base for artistic work. Much effort is put into making elaborate elements around courtyards— just like the ones on the front facade. A *zharookha* with exquisite carvings is often placed on the street-side facade; but an equally well-carved one could be found looking over the courtyard.

Building material had much to do, both with the organisation of architectural spaces and with the aesthetic treatment of facades, elements and surfaces. Stone has been a very important building material in Rajasthan. However, stone is primarily used for a trabeated system of construction and not arcuated, although at first sight most of the openings appear to be of an arched shape. There is a close relationship between the patterns of spatial organisation and the structural system responsible for carrying loads. The supports consisting of columns and pillars with bases, capitals, brackets, beams and roofs are all made in stone, but with a varying degree of carvings depending upon what the owner of the house could afford.

All these structural elements along with spatial elements like *zharookhas* and *chhatris* are pre-carved from stone with a predetermined assembly system. They could be carved on the site of the work or even ordered outside and brought to the site for assembly. Even today the system is working, and the *slats*, the stone-carvers of some areas like Jaisalmer, are well-known for their carving work.

Fig. 8 Interior space in a Jaisalmer haveli (cf Fig. 6), showing a courtyard

Zharookhas and certain other elements are exported not only to other parts of the country, but even out of the country. It is like a kit of parts which can be taken anywhere and assembled.

Because of the structural limitations inherent in stone elements like columns and beams, large spans are not used in the architecture of Rajasthan. Spatial organisation is therefore governed by this limitation. Wherever larger spaces are made, they are filled in with columns. Walls are also used along with the column and beam system. Because of this system of construction, large unobstructed spaces are not found in the architecture of Rajasthan. Also the system uses simple rectilinear geometry where the organisation of a space is based on squares and rectangles (Fig. 8).

Construction and related expression

As already discussed, a very well-developed system of construction, based on the idea of kits of various parts and their predetermined patterns of assembly, was developed in Rajasthan. In may ways it parallels similar systems developed elsewhere, at times using wood as the basic material, as in Gujarat. The sophistication of the system demanded a definite language resulting in well-expressed manifestations of the built form.

In this section of the chapter we are attempting to understand the direct relationship between the construction system and the aesthetic expression. The principal elements used are discussed below.

Both round columns and square pillars are fairly common. However, generally the free-standing supports are round, whereas the ones attached to walls are square or rectangular—more like pilasters. One can also find a square pillar with semicircular pilasters attached to the pillars. While the support system required for structural purposes is obvious, the treatment of these elements can vary from the plain and simple to the very elaborate and exquisite, depending upon the social and economic status of the owner of the house. Besides their structural responsibility, these elements offer a good base for carving and other decorative treatment. All columns invariably sit on a base, also made of stone. Even in parts of Gujarat where the column or pillar shaft is wooden, the base is always in stone. The base is, in the majority of cases, shaped like a bell, though one can also find the use of a flattened sphere, as well as water pots.

There are important structural elements which help in transferring all loads: from beams to brackets to capitals and finally to columns or pillars. As mentioned earlier, these are prefabricated and pre-carved elements which, when assembled, present a highly articulated and well-integrated whole. They too can be intricately carved, depending upon the status of the owner. Like the bases, the capitals can also be shaped to follow a bell shape, a flattened sphere or a pot. Amongst these structural elements the bracket has a very special place. It helps in transferring the load from a horizontal member like a beam to the vertical column. These brackets are invariably shaped like arches, but structurally they are not arches, and have often been wrongly interpreted: they are made by the articulation of two brackets with other structural elements, and are foliated with various cusps. A carved pipal leaf invariably crowns the openings, making it more auspicious. Stone beams are supported from capital to capital with these brackets providing additional support and reducing the effective span. In houses where the decorative treatment is elaborate, the beams also provide additional surfaces for carving or painting. On external surfaces, even in courtyards, a beam also provides a base for *chhajjas*. The *chhajja* is an extremely important climatic element necessary to provide shade to openings, as well as to external surfaces. It helps in reducing the radiation through the surfaces of the building. Along with some other

Fig. 9 Havelis in Sikar, Shekhavati District

elements, *chhajjas* also play a dominating role in facade-making in the architecture of Rajasthan. Many of these elements have become inseparable parts of the visual expression in these buildings (Figs 9, 10).

The architecture of Rajasthan cannot be imagined without the *zharookhas*. It has almost become a symbol of the state's traditional architecture. Functionally, a *zharookha* is an element permitting discreet participation with the outside. In all houses this part is made with extra care. To the outside world is it a show-piece, an expression of wealth for the owners of the house; for the inside, it is a 'place' which offers an opportunity to draw light, ventilation and provide a view. Still, it maintains privacy for the women of the house. It is structured on the facade with the use of geometric articulation, along with other elements. Generally the *zharookhas* are used in upper floors where they project out over the street. In *havelis* and larger houses, the projections increase as one moves up.

Intense heat and strong light have forced the *baris* (windows) to be small. One can find a small window set directly in the wall, but in most

Fig. 10 Detail of the Aath Haveli complex, Nawalgarh

cases a *bari* is a part of the *zharookha* (Fig. 1). The designers of these facades recognised the limitations of small windows and therefore, invariably, a *bari* is made a part of a larger element. When not integrated with a *zharookha*, it is part of a larger carved panel. A *bari* may be surrounded by delicate trelliswork in stone as in Jaisalmer, or it may be punched in a plain stone slab, as in Udaipur. An interesting aspect of the *zharookha* and the *bari* is that, besides their functional role, they play an important decorative role, and are often used as miniaturised motifs.

The *chhatri* is also a very dominant element and its application can be seen in a variety of ways. At times it is used as a functional element, but by and large its use is aesthetic or symbolic. A *chhatri* is a semi-open element; open on the sides and covered on top. It can be considered as close to a cupola. The most commonly used plan forms are square, octagonal and round. A very important aspect of its use is the manipulation of the skyline. It can be put on top of any building. In their larger manifestations, they are used as cenotaphs. Like *zharookhas*, the *chhatris* are the most extensively used elements from the kit of architectural elements. Even on a complete building, one can bring a *chhatri* from a *slat* and add it to the roof. A very important aspect of the architecture of Rajasthan is the manner in which the skyline is treated. *Chhatris*, *chhajjas*, finials and crenellated parapets are used. Several permutations and combinations of these elements could be used in the assembly of houses. One can observe a variety of design attitudes in these elements. One could find extensive use of the Bengal type of *chhatri* at one place as compared with simpler ones at another. It is not uncommon to find the use of *zharookhas* and *chhatris* in combination.

Expressions independent of construction

Although the logic of construction and the nature of building materials demand certain aesthetic expressions, it does not always so happen. The idea of the 'little more' than the needed is always present; and it extends into the functional as well as the structural aspects of the built form. If the philosophy of modern architecture, which advocates purity of construction and honesty of expression, were to be used for evaluating the manifest form of the architecture of Rajasthan, then many visual expressions would appear fake or superfluous (Fig. 11).

Starting with the fenestrations in the facade, it is interesting to compare the actual openings in the surface with the appearance of openings. Due to climatic as well as privacy reasons, the windows are actually very small, but they are integrated with larger stone panels which may be simple or elaborate in their treatment. Here the important aspect is the creation of this larger surface around the openings in order to manage the geometric subdivisions of the surface of the facade. Not only this, but the rich would elaborately carve the entire stone panel. Obviously, this defies the logical scrutiny used in understanding relationships between form and function. It could even be called camouflaging. However, the judgment of aesthetic expressions in architecture cannot be based on any one philosophical attitude.

Similarly, if the logic of structural forms were to be applied to the elements evolved in the architecture of Rajasthan, then many of the elements would appear manipulated and not true to the honest form. The most outstanding example is the appearance of the arched openings. Actually these openings are not made by the construction of true arches: they are created by putting together two stone brackets shaped to look like arches. Further, the shape of these brackets is cusped. Both the shaping of the arch and the cusping are purely for visual reasons and have no structural role to play. The structural role is played by the brackets which belong to the trabeated system of construction and not to the arcuate one, though it appears to be the latter. Occasionally one does come across true arches, generally on larger openings; these have been influenced by Islamic methods of construction and are more common in later periods.

These arch-shaped openings with their varied number of cusps, have almost become a trade mark in this built form. This 'archway' and the *zharookha* when put together conjure up images of architecture which belongs nowhere except Rajasthan. These images, over a period of time, must have become so strong that they started finding expressions in other media and other materials. An important aspect of aesthetic expression is the idea of visual continuity of images. Such a continuity of visual imagery can be seen in several other vernacular traditions also. Architectural elements, generated as a result of building materials and a particular construction technology, are replicated in other materials and by using other methods of construction. The most interesting example is, of course, the stone brackets which are shaped as arches and are imitated in brick, wood, mud and even fabric. Sometimes it is difficult even to recognise the origin of such elements, or the original material. Whether the shapes were first created in wood, stone or fabric remains unresolved. While the available evidence shows the use in building construction from much earlier times, the fabric examples are of much later times, when such images formed parts of

Fig. 11 A street facade in Jaipur, showing lower level shops and residences above; and Western motifs in the decoration

tents and other cloth shelters. Miniature paintings which show the use of such features in tents are of the seventeenth and eighteenth centuries, though this does not mean that they were not used earlier.

In conclusion, it can be said that the rich and elaborate architecture of Rajasthan has developed a very systematic way of building. It has a well-developed language in which the building components are prefabricated and are available with *slats*, the stone-carvers. These elements provide a strong sense of continuity of form and are part of a consistent theme within which variations are made. In the process, the identity of the basic character is preserved while numerous variations are actually achieved. It is also found that this thematic expression has led to certain visual images which find a place in the aesthetic expression of this architecture. To a great extent this attitude continues, and several new buildings make use of traditional elements— particularly the *zharookha*, the *chhatri* and the *chhajja*.

---

[1] Andrew Topsfield, *Paintings from Rajasthan: National Gallery of Victoria* (Melbourne, 1980), p.7.

Chapter Eight

A TALE OF TWO CITIES:
HOUSE AND TOWN IN INDIA TODAY

Sunand Prasad

In many old north Indian cities one can see evidence of two distinct paradigms of urban fabric. One could be called 'traditional' and the other 'modern', or one 'Indian' and the other 'Western'. This and similar conditions in cities in the Middle East and North Africa—for example the 'casbah' versus the colonial settlement—have often been remarked on in terms of the contrasting figure ground relationship of space and built form. It is now commonplace for architects, urbanists and critics to remark on the virtues of the traditional paradigm but the reality is that it has a vanishingly small status in determining the shape of the rapid urbanisation currently in progress. It would be useful to understand the precise reasons for the change of paradigms and to assess what role the two paradigms should play and are likely to play in future development of cities. This chapter tries to clear some ground in the pursuit of these goals.

Contemporary urban Indian culture accords a low status to the traditional paradigm.[1] Those people who have the economic freedom to choose are deciding, on the whole overwhelmingly, against living in the old or traditional parts of the city and prefer the newer areas. They explain their choice in strongly physical terms. To describe the two kinds of urban fabric as they may be experienced is therefore a promising starting point, so I give below narratives of two 'journeys' one can undertake in Delhi, together with commentaries on them.

Journey One: Shahjahanabad (established 1648)[2]

Standing on the roof terrace of a house on the hillock called Pahadi Bhojla in the Walled City of Delhi and looking out towards the Jama Masjid which, atop its own hillock, dominates the city, one can see spread out into the distance, what seems to be a single contiguous mass of building (Fig.1). Accidents of alignment might indicate streets and lanes otherwise hidden. The occasional *peepal* tree suggests that there are other interstices that bring light and air into the dense mass. The roofs, all flat, are heavily used, almost as if they were the ground.

Fig. 1 View over Shahjahanabad

Children play, clothes are dried, food and bodies sunned, kites flown and pigeons fancied. There are even shacks on the roof exactly like independent huts on the ground. Looking closely one can see that the city is made up of houses built round courtyards and arranged, close-packed, along narrow lanes which lead to wider bazaar streets.

In this city is apparent a three-level hierarchy of routes. The primary axes of the city which connect the main gates and the palace or important temple are wide (30m-40m) and straight (Fig.2). Aside from their part in the circulation system, these have a processional use and honorific status. Originally, important public institutions and the houses of those closest to the throne or important in civic life, or of rich merchants, would be situated there. There would also be shops and emporia, sometimes in arcades as in Delhi and Jaipur. The secondary bazaar streets lined with shops, workshops and warehouses form the main circulation system of the city (Fig.3). These are narrower (5m-12m) and through generally straight, are not rigorously so. Above and behind the shops and workshops are houses. Finally, the *galis* (lanes) of

Fig. 2 Chandni Chowk, Shahjahanabad

Fig. 3 Bazaar street in the old city

the *mohallas* (neighbourhoods), are the 'capillaries' of the system.[3] These are quite narrow (1m-5m) and winding, and connect to the bazaar (Fig.4). These would on the whole be residential though there may be the occasional workshop or shop as part of the house. Since *mohallas* are associated with occupation, some *galis* may be predominantly commercial at the lower level. The *galis* often have dead ends which means that the *mohallas* are not generally through-routes. Only those familiar with the area would know which *galis* lead out of the *mohalla*. A strong element of security against the stranger is thus built into the system. The *mohalla* is the dominant form of neighbourhood but not the only one. The *katra*, for example, is a smaller neighbourhood unit, centred usually on a single space, found in the walled city of Delhi.[4]

   This three-level hierarchy applies particularly to capital cities like Delhi, Jaipur and Udaipur. Medium-sized towns like Saharanpur and Kankhal may combine the first two levels. What is common to all traditional urban settlements is the morphology of the *mohalla*.

Descending through the house and into the narrow lane—the *gali*—and walking down to the bazaar one would notice that the various streets of the city—from the quiet, ten-foot-wide *gali* to the crowded and noisy sixty-foot-wide bazaar that leads to the mosque—seem to harbour a great variety of human activity. While the centre of the wider streets is devoted to traffic, human and animal as well as mechanical, other activities take priority near the edges and in the narrower *galis*. People meet, talk, buy, sell, manufacture, eat, cook and play. Most human activities necessary for sustaining life, except the most private ones, are exercised here openly.

   The public realm—the main streets, *galis*, junctions, nodes, *chowks*—in this system is multi-functional and multivalent. It is multi-functional in the sense that the streets are not just routes, but places for commercial exchange; for meeting and encounter; or, simply, for being in, for relaxation and pleasure in company. It is multivalent in the sense that any one space has different values attached to it—a patch of it may be sacred; a route may take on a particular significance on a particular occasion. There may be a procession on a holy day through a bazaar which then would cease to be the realm of commerce and become a space of ritual and public theatre. In a *mohalla* or *katra* the street is to the houses what the courtyard is to the rooms in a house. At a community function like a wedding this quality of the street is intensified: it becomes a communal courtyard; the city *becomes* the house.

Transactions between the house and the street are frequent. There has been a strong tradition in homes of eating freshly-cooked food from the bazaar. In this instance the street serves as a kitchen. At weddings— which play a very big role in social life—itinerant teams of caterers set up in the available space nearest to the house. From one of these 'kitchen camps' two thousand guests might be fed. Marriages have auspicious seasons and so at times neighbourhoods may be quite full with giant cooking-pots on the streets, lodged in what to an outsider may seem at first to be pointless widenings and twists of the *galis*.

Beneath the riot of advertising hoardings, telegraph and electricity poles and the general squalor, a distinct order is perceptible. This very public realm is contained by continuous walls of buildings on each side. On the wider bazaar streets there are successive layers in front of the plane of these street walls: shops; retractable extensions from shops; and vendors selling from barrows or mats on the ground. The buildings that form the 'street walls' in the *mohalla* are generally houses, but in between there will be temples, *dharmashalas* (pilgrim hostelries), madrasas (Islamic schools) and other institutions and public buildings. The typological differences are often small and subtle.

Nodes in the traditional urban street system have special meanings. Temples and mosques and other important buildings may be situated at junctions. The word for courtyard, *chowk*, is also used for the space formed at the crossing of roads, evidence for its importance as a *place*. Apart from particular places formed at junctions, the secondary and tertiary streets have frequent, irregularly spaced, widenings. These may be associated, for example, with the sacred *peepal* tree, a public well or a shrine.

The street cross-section of the *mohalla* provides psychological as well as physical shelter. On the psychological level, spatial enclosure of the kind that built-up streets and squares provide intensifies what might be called the 'urban charge', provided certain other conditions are met; namely that people should feel reasonably secure and that there should be a reason for being in the space other than transiently. Often the enclosure itself creates these conditions—a space overlooked by a number of houses and other buildings is likely to be safer, and the contents of the buildings themselves may provide the reasons for being in the space. Over and above these factors, however, there seems to be a value simply in the spatial fact of enclosure. Is it a counterpart to the

Fig. 4 A *gali* in the walled city of Delhi

psychological shelter of the room? Is it more related to orientation and
legibility? The traditional bazaar and *gali* provide such sheltering and
legible urban space.

On the physical level the cross-section of the typical *gali* ameliorates the climatic conditions in two ways. Firstly, for most of the day it is possible to find some shade and so escape the direct heat of the sun. Lightweight canopies and awnings, reaching right across the narrow *gali*, provide further shade. Secondly, the buildings enjoy a high degree of mutual shading which reduces the incident sunshine on the walls, confining much of it to the roofs which then reflect a significant portion back to the sky. The large thermal mass of the buildings means that their temperature rises relatively slowly, which has the effect of attenuating the diurnal variation in temperature both within the

Fig. 5   The entrance to a haveli in Old Delhi

buildings and, crucially, in the street. Temperature measurements taken in Delhi and in Jaisalmer have indicated that the air temperature in the *mohalla* and bazaar streets is approximately 2°C less in the hottest weather than the air temperature in open spaces, these open spaces being in the new parts of town in Delhi or outside the city walls in Jaisalmer.[5]

When the ambient air temperature is above 40°C, a reduction of 2°C is significant in terms of comfort. It explains why many of the bazaars in the traditional city remain active, if subdued, even in the hottest part of the day at the hottest time of the year. In short, the morphology makes it physically possible for people to move about the city.

Individual buildings are signalled along the street wall by elaborate doorways all on a similar basic pattern, often with overhanging balconies above (Fig.5). The elaborateness is functional as well as ornamental. The building gives physical shelter to the street and provides public places to sit, elevated above the dirt and the hubbub. It also gives signals about the residents. A number of architectural devices on the house front modulate the street edge and activate the boundary between the house and the street.

The following are some of the architectural devices on the interface between building and street:

1. The *chabootara* (or *ota* in Rajasthani): this is a raised platform placed along the whole or part of the street frontage, interrupted by the flight of steps that give to the front door. This platform is available for anyone's use for resting or sitting on, or for sunning oneself in the winter. The raised position makes for a clear separation from the street while allowing a flexible degree of interaction with it. It is not unknown for sellers of vegetables or trinkets to set up here. In some places, like Jaisalmer, the residents of the house will sleep on it at night when the street becomes a collective 'bedroom'.

2. The *gokhas*: these are two square platforms of approximately seat dimension at seat height, on either side of the door and within the entrance arch. They may be found in houses with or without the outer *chabootara*. They too are free for use by strangers for sitting on or for resting a load.

3. The entrance arch: the front door is commonly set at the back of a large arched niche which can be sheltered in during rain.

4. The *chajjas*: these are permanent overhanging canopies on the façade supported on brackets or struts. They are generally of stone though corrugated-iron ones are also seen. They give shade to the

façade but can also shelter people from the sun and rain. In some houses *chajjas* project successively further out on upper storeys, almost meeting across the street at the top. In such cases the street may be almost fully sheltered.

5. Balconies, galleries, *jharokhas* and *gokhras*: these project from the upper storeys of houses and are all devices which make it possible for people to be between the street and the house; to be in the room and yet physically over the street and able to look along it. *Jharokhas* are open, aedicular, bays with columns and roofs—reminiscent of, but more elaborate than, oriels. They often have *jalis*—carved stonework or timber screens—that permit one to look out without being seen. *Ghokhras* are a particularly Udaipuri device. All these devices are simultaneously part of the street and of the house. They connect the house with the street at the upper storeys and at the same time provide privacy to the rooms by making a screen in front of the window wall. Like *chajjas* they also shelter the house, the street and people from sun and rain.

6. *Alas*: an *ala*, also called a *taak*, is a niche or alcove in the wall. It is rare to find a street façade without two or more of these. Their particular contribution to the street seems to have been to provide a place for an oil lamp that lit a part of the street while lighting the entrance to the house. The advent of electrical light has made this practice redundant, and nowadays this only happens at *diwali* in some towns.

These various devices are found in different combinations in houses. Some houses, like those in one of the best-kept of the Old Delhi streets, the wealthy Jain Naughara, have all of them. The devices play a strong part in the ordering, composition and expression of the elevation. The *chabootara* and the balcony are the base and cornice of the tripartite ordering of many of the houses. The alcoves and *chajjas* are frequently used as compositional elements. *Jharokhas* and *chajjas* are placed symmetrically above the door and speak of its importance.

Beyond their physical and compositional functions, some of these devices also have a symbolic function either directly or as settings. Thus in a Hindu house the entrance arch will almost invariably contain a statue of Ganesh above the door. In the same place a Muslim house may have the number '786' which is a numeric code for 'In the name of Allah, Most Gracious, Most Merciful'.[6] There may be frescoes— invariably fading from neglect—showing scenes and figures from the epics or family history, set in niches and panels. The lavishness and quality of the front would express the status and culture of the family.

Fig. 6 A courtyard in a haveli in Old Delhi

Through the elaborate portal of a typical house is visible only a dim
hallway with a glimmer of daylight at the far end. The hallway which
will often have a 'dog-leg' plan leads into a courtyard (Fig.6). This
may be quite small, sometimes merely a light well, or very large;
whatever its size it will feel calm and sheltering. On axis with the
entrance may be the main room or *dalaan*, with smaller rooms in the
side ranges (Fig.7). Especially in their deeper recesses, these spaces,
cool and dark, shut out the glare and the hot bustle of the bazaar. In
traditional households the use of only a few rooms—bathroom, kitchen,
stores—is fixed; the others are used variably for sitting, working,

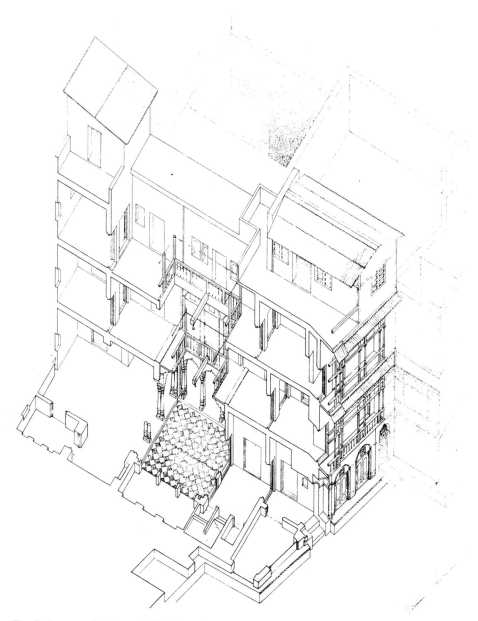

Fig. 7 Cutaway drawing of a Delhi haveli

sleeping, gathering and eating; and differently in different weather. If
there are upper storeys, there will be another large room over the
entrance, frequently with a gallery overhanging the doorway and
overlooking the street: a zone in between the house and the world
outside, both connecting and separating. Continuing on up through the
house one will reach one of the roof terraces that one looked out over
from Pahadi Bhojla.

The basic component of the city fabric is a courtyard house. In its refined form, from Gujarat to West Bengal, such a house is known as a *haveli*. The traditional city is made of haveli-type houses.

The relatively wealthy will have a whole house and may have tenants in its peripheral parts. From about 1960 onwards there was an exodus of middle-class people—merchants and professionals—from the walled city of Delhi. They settled in the 'colonies' as the new neighbourhoods are called. The houses they left either became converted to commercial or industrial use, or became entirely tenanted, often in extremely crowded conditions, by relatively poor people. A similar process has taken place in other cities, though the social and functional mix in the old city may be different. The walled city of Delhi has experienced the most extreme pressures of commercialisation, congestion, poverty and communal strife.

Journey Two: New Delhi (established 1911)

If, instead of looking north over the old city from Pahadi Bhojla, one flew up and looked to the south over New Delhi, a very different image of a city would present itself. Rather than the occasional tree in the mass of buildings, one would see detached buildings or groups or rows of buildings seemingly set amongst trees (Fig.8). The streets here are much wider and the buildings are set back from the street edge. Travelling south the buildings are at first mainly institutional and commercial, but then give way to the empty, leafy boulevards of Lutyens's Delhi with villas set in capacious grounds. Beyond this, one comes to the modern residential 'colonies' of desirable south Delhi.[7] The roads are still wide and clean and tree-lined, if not so lavishly. There are few people to be seen and the road is plainly devoted to motor transport (Fig.9).

Like the old city, the new city has its axes and processional routes (Fig.10). However, the road system of the colonies is quite unlike that of the traditional city in respects other than its function as circulation. Shopping is concentrated in 'markets' or shopping centres and is not linear and city-wide. Industrial and commercial uses are zoned and segregated from housing and retail. Thus the urban public realm is attenuated in comparison with the traditional city. Political assemblies and state processions of the largest scale take place along the central ceremonial boulevards. On a more everyday level, a road may be closed temporarily for a wedding, but this is a defiance of the urban morphology—the necessary enclosure has to be provided by making large tents over the roadway.

Fig. 8 A house amongst trees in a wealthy colony

In the colonies, the streets are relatively quiet and uncongested. There are rarely any obstructions to the passage of motor traffic, although the volume of traffic itself causes congestion. Services work better than they do in the old city. Even in the newest and least affluent neighbourhoods, there is more greenery than in the old city. Roads are often tree-lined. There is no nuisance to houses from noise, fumes or danger from industrial neighbours as there is in the old city, although there is a general problem of pollution levels. There are places for children to play in the open air, and it is possible to take peaceful strolls near one's home.

Fig. 9 A road in a colony

Fig. 10 The central vista, Vijay Chowk, New Delhi

The houses are set back from the carriageway which they address with a vigorous, even violent, individuality; even if they are in rows, attached to their neighbours on both sides (Fig.11). Each has a wide gate to a short driveway and beside the gate-post the owner's name in large letters, often back-lit at night. Beside the drive is a small lawn. The entrance door to the house, somewhere at the end of the drive, is relatively insignificant.

With the houses set well back from the edges of the streets, openness rather than enclosure is the dominant characteristic of the outdoors. Climatically no shelter can be afforded to the street by the houses and in most colonies the road is inhospitable in the summer during the day; a condition made worse by the large expanses of black, heat-absorbing and radiating asphalt. However, the most mature and wealthy of the colonies show how dense tree planting can provide both shade and a modified microclimate as good as that of the old city. Cool air-streams due to evaporative cooling are established in well-treed areas. Temperature measurements confirm that the differentials are of the same order as those between the Old City streets and bare open spaces.[8]

Fig. 11 A colony house front addressing the street

In the colony, the house expresses itself to the public realm as an object, set back from it. An upper balcony may look out over the street. The wall or hedgerow, a gate and a nameplate will make the edge of the street. The car on the drive glimpsed through the gate is an essential part of the scene—the equivalent perhaps of the elaborate portal of the older tradition (Fig.12). Over the relatively plain entrance door there may be a statue of Ganesh—or in Muslim houses the figures '786'. The whole is arguably as redolent with symbolism as the entrance to a *haveli*-type house. The difference is that the house makes no functional contribution to the public realm, other than the reassurance of the existence of habitation.

Fig. 12 The car in the gated drive of a villa

Fig. 13 Villa interior

Inside, the house has a set of rooms on the European pattern—dining-, living- and bedrooms (Fig.13). The house looks out to the front lawn or a back yard rather than into a courtyard. Instead of a courtyard, there is usually a small light-well (a product of bye-laws, like the front and rear set-backs) to allow the deep plan to work—to let the bathrooms and kitchens in the centre have some light and ventilation. In the rooms there will usually be air conditioners or desert coolers. On the first floor there may be a balcony overlooking the lawn and street, full of house plants (Fig.14). The design of the house suggests that a high value has been given to space, light and greenery and display.

The dominant house type here is based on the villa—a detached house set in its own grounds. These are the houses of the relatively very wealthy. Not all of wealthy south Delhi is made up of houses on plots with lawns—many people live in blocks of flats—but the design of these flats subscribes to the same values as the villas. The flats look outwards; they are made of rooms with specific uses; space, light and

Fig. 14 A villa balcony overlooking greenery

greenery are highly cherished; the spaces in between buidings are not intended for habitation. Most of the people here would prefer to live in a villa if they could afford one in a satisfactory location.

Here and there in pockets and backlands one might find a squatter's colony of the really poor, but one has to go further out towards the edges of the city to find the places where live the people officially described as belonging to the MIGs and LIGs ('middle or lower income groups')—below which are the EWSs ('economically weaker sections'), below whom are the anonymous, unlabelled, often itinerant, resilient communities clinging on the side of urban India like barnacles to a ship's hull. Housing for the MIG and LIG groups follows the pattern of the houses and flats seen in south Delhi, but with progressively reduced standards of space and material provision.[9] Only at the lowest level of official provision of housing are courtyards again thought suitable, and mixed use of rooms accepted on the grounds of economic necessity.

Two Paradigms

In order to concentrate on morphology, I have deliberately omitted
some features which have a powerful effect both on the perception, and
on the actual experience, of living in the two areas of the city. The
traditional city has very high population densities (up to 2,000 people
per hectare in some areas with many sleeping on the street). It has
pollutant industries adjacent to housing. It is unsanitary and poorly
maintained. There is serious traffic congestion. Building and
development practice is poorly regulated, causing encroachments by
private buildings onto public land and roadways. In many cases there is
a complete breakdown of a civic regime. Thus the two paradigms do
not present themselves in a form that allows them to be evaluated for
their virtues as functional responses to the problems and opportunities
of living in the city. They have to be 'mentally cleaned up'.

The two paradigms have been identified above respectively as the
haveli type and the villa type.[10] The figure-ground diagram (Fig. 15)
summarises the difference between the paradigmatic house types in the

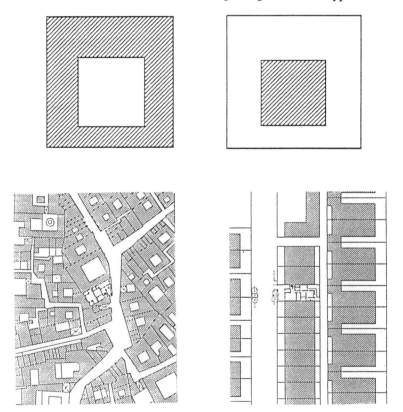

Fig. 15 Haveli: Villa (above); Mohalla: Colony (below)

two parts of the city; and the urban morphologies that the two types predicate can be depicted by map fragments of the two types of neighbourhood, the *mohalla* and the 'colony'.

In the above commentary we noted the following comparative characteristics:

Haveli	*Villa*
enclosed/sheltering	open
inward looking	outward looking
multivalency of space and place	specific meanings
multi-functional use of spaces	specific uses for spaces
gardens amongst buildings	buildings amongst gardens
urban	suburban

In talking to residents, including those who have experience of both types, associations like the following are made:[11]

congested	free flowing
dirty	clean
regressive	progressive
communal	individual
cool	hot
secure	insecure (danger of burglary)

One can also make technical and social comparisons, such as:

foot/animal	motor car
extended family	nuclear family

The first paradigm has existed in the Indian subcontinent for at least five thousand years and has a continuous history of use. The morphology of the Indus valley cities (circa 2500-1000 BC) was based on the courtyard house. So was the morphology of the early Aryan cities, of great cities of the Buddhist period like Taxila and Pataliputra, and of later Indo-Islamic cities up to the colonial era.

The second paradigm can be traced to settlements the British built for themselves near, but quite separate from, the native city. Typically there would be a military 'Cantonment' and a 'Civil Lines'. The urban fabric was of well-planted compounds with free-standing bungalows accessed by lanes. The bungalow itself had been developed in the very early years of the colonial era by combining the building-to-land relationship and interior arrangement of the villa with the climatic and material qualities of the Bengali cottage or 'Bangla'.[12]

The decline of the courtyard house form and of the traditional city can be traced from the gathering popularity—amongst Indians now as well as the colonists—of the bungalow from the late nineteenth century onward. It is not possible here to go into why and how this happened, but we will accept that the culture of the colonial rulers had an overwhelming effect on those they ruled.

The British, though they were impressed by grand Indian monuments and craftsmanship, with a few exceptions regarded the native city as dirty, dangerous and hostile. Their treatment of Shahjahanabad is well known: the clearance of the grand *havelis* near the Red Fort to allow clear lines of fire; and the bringing of the railway into the heart of the city, over great gardens. The early urbanist Patrick Geddes was the only influential voice to champion native urban form. In a series of reports on Indian towns around 1915 to 1919, he developed his notion of 'conservative surgery'—keeping the sheltering, place-making, many layered qualities of the narrow lanes and courtyards while improving traffic flow and sanitation with judicious and finely-tailored projects of demolition and reconstruction. But some thirty years later, and after the end of the colonial era, his friend the architect H.V. Lanchester was to write:

> [The] courtyard plan has advantages in a hot climate, giving shade and protection from dust storms—as anyone who has suffered from these in a bungalow can testify. Taking everything into account however, bungalows are healthier dwellings. A good many Indians are beginning to live in them.[13]

It is striking that the real eclipse of the traditional ('Indian') paradigm and the ascendency of the modern ('Western') one has taken place after independence and at an increasing pace. Until the 1960s many parts of the walled city of Delhi were desirable addresses for professional and business people. The exodus of this class of people from the old city gathered pace in the late 1960s and 1970s and by the 1980s it would have been a rare upper middle-class old Delhi family which had not built a new house out in the 'colonies'. The picture in other north Indian cities is similar.

A combination of official policy action and inaction after independence effectively removed the traditional paradigm from continuing use in determining the shape of new settlements. For example, building bye-laws, particularly as they relate to widths of houses and set-backs, make it impossible to build courtyard houses in close-packed configurations. The lack of enforcement of planning laws in the old parts of cities has made them progressively more congested and more blighted by polluting industries and commercial uses. The absence of any preservation legislation or conservation mechanism other than in archaeological terms means that, given the pressures, there is little to prevent the decay of traditional houses and neighbourhoods to a point where it becomes difficult for most people to see any quality in them even if they want to. Only very recently, within the last fifteen years, have some architects and urbanists begun to champion qualities of the traditional paradigm.

In many ways the ascendancy of a new idea about urban fabric at the expense of a traditional one parallels changes in the West driven by the revolution in the modes of production and the coming of modern industry. For example, the development of motorised transport, the changes in patterns of work and changes in family structure are important parts of the picture. It is arguable that the decay of the traditional city, both literally and as a model, is simply part of a global phenomenon of urban growth and the idealisation of suburban life-styles, rather than a rejection of indigenous forms induced by the colonial experience. If this is true, we could expect to see, as in the West, a general return to favour of traditional forms, the accumulation of a recorded body of knowledge about them, and the development of critical awareness to help guide policy and design. There are indications that some of these are taking place but in a very small way, insufficient to keep pace with the destruction of examples of traditional fabric. So while there are parallels with the changes that attended industrialisation in the West, what is taking place in India has distinct characteristics.

At the same time, however, to distinguish the two paradigms as 'Indian' and 'Western' does not help to explain why the latter is so dominant in India today. 'Indian' is often used in this context to imply authenticity, which is of questionable logic and seems to imply that the 'modern' cannot be 'Indian'.

There are other problems with the Indian/Western distinction. The traditional city represents an Indian paradigm of the art of making cities. It does not follow that it is uniquely or entirely Indian. The *haveli* has its equivalent in *palazzi* and other European courtyard types which can be traced via Pompeiian atrium houses and Greek *agoras* to a likely common Mesopotamian origin. Conversely, the house in the clearing, the village cottage, are as much part of Indian culture as the *haveli*. The bungalow derives from the Bengali cottage, albeit shorn of its yard and now built away from its original cultural and climatic context. So, while the *haveli* has a long history of indigenous development, and the villa clearly owes a great deal to Western models, the simply distinction—Indian versus Western—obscures more than enlightens. They are both now Indian paradigms, though they could still be distinguished, roughly, as the traditional and the modern.

It is difficult to compare the two as responses to the problems and possibilities of living in a modern city because most examples of the 'traditional' form are severely blighted by poor maintenance, inadequate sanitation, congestion and lack of regulation of development. Furthermore, the development of the traditional paradigm had ceased by the time of independence. Official policy since independence has hugely favoured the 'modern' paradigm, and the 'traditional' one has received very little documentation or critical evaluation. Urban neighbourhoods built on the traditional paradigm are in danger of extinction. It is therefore essential to conserve and document the traditional form on as large a scale as possible.

On a small scale architects are studying and experimenting with it, adapting it successfully to present circumstances. A number of recent developments suggest a future for the traditional paradigm. With the latest developments in communication, home and work are being reintegrated. Planning ideology has shifted away from rigid functional zoning of cities to mixed use, with pollutant and heavy traffic-generating industry being sited away from cities. High-density, low-rise building is recognised as being an effective response to urban housing and ancillary uses. The motor car is becoming smaller again. Perhaps an ancient paradigm will organise the city fabric of the future.

---

[1] Sunand Prasad, 'The Havelis of north India', unpublished PhD thesis, Royal College of Art, London, 1988. Much of this paper is based on the research material gathered for the thesis.

[2] The walled city of Delhi (formally named Shahjahanabad, after the Emperor Shahjahan who ordered its building) is the major part of an area which has been called Delhi since New Delhi has existed.

[3] *Mohalla*, Urdu (also Persian and Arabic, *mahalla*) = neighbourhood. Usually self-contained and encloseable.

[4] A *katra* is a neighbourhood 'in which a number of households live in tenements or houses with an enclosed space with one common entrance': Harshad R. Trivedi, *Housing and Community in Old Delhi: the Katra form of urban settlement* (Delhi, 1980). A dictionary of 1958 defines it as 'a small market square' which is more faithful to the original meaning of the word (*Sankshipt Hindi Shabdasagar* (Benares, 1958.) For practical purposes a *katra* nowadays is a small *mohalla*, usually associated with a single communal space—most commonly a narrow street or courtyard—with a lesser or greater number of shops, warehouses and other working places.

[5] S. Prasad, 'The Havelis of north India'.

[6] 'Bismillah Rehman Rahim.'

[7] Examples of south Delhi suburbs are New Friends Colony, Defence Colony and Kalindi Colony.

[8] S. Prasad, 'The Havelis of north India'.

[9] This housing is not necessarily for rent—the Delhi Development Authority, for example, is involved in allocation of land for sale to developers, groups and individuals, as well as in the construction of housing for rent.

[10] The equivalent of the Court and the Pavilion building type as often used in morphological studies, for example, the work of Land Use and Built Form Studies at Cambridge in the early 1970s.

[11] S. Prasad, 'The Havelis of north India'.

[12] Anthony D. King, *The Bungalow: the production of a global culture* (London, 1984).

[13] Jacqueline Tyrwhitt (ed.), *Patrick Geddes in India* (preface by H.V. Lanchester) (London, 1947).